D1384798

RHYMES *of a*
RED CROSS MAN

By

ROBERT W. SERVICE

Author of
"Songs of a Sourdough," "Ballads of a Cheechako,"
"Rhymes of a Rolling Stone," and
"The Trail of '98"

TORONTO:
WILLIAM BRIGGS
1916

To the Memory of
My Brother

LIEUTENANT ALBERT SERVICE

Canadian Infantry

Killed in Action.   France, August, 1916

FOREWORD

I've tinkered at my bits of rhymes
In weary, woeful, waiting times;
In doleful hours of battle-din,
Ere yet they brought the wounded in;
Through vigils of the fateful night,
In lousy barns by candle-light;
In dug-outs, sagging and aflood,
On stretchers stiff and bleared with blood;
By ragged grove, by ruined road,
By hearths accurst where Love abode;
By broken altars, blackened shrines
I've tinkered at my bits of rhymes.

I've solaced me with scraps of song
The desolated ways along;
Through sickly fields all shrapnel-sown,
And meadows reaped by death alone;
By blazing cross and splintered spire,
By headless Virgin in the mire;
By gardens gashed amid their bloom,
By gutted grave, by shattered tomb;

7

FOREWORD

Beside the dying and the dead,
Where rocket green and rocket red,
In trembling pools of poising light,
With flowers of flame festoon the night.
Ah me! by what dark ways of wrong
I've cheered my heart with scraps of song.

So here's my sheaf of war-won verse,
And some is bad—and some is worse.
And if at times I curse a bit,
You needn't read that part of it;
For through it all like horror runs
The red resentment of the guns.
And you yourself would mutter when
You took the things that once were men,
And sped them through that zone of hate
To where the dripping surgeons wait;
And wonder, too, if in God's sight
War ever, ever can be right.

Yet may it not be, crime and war
But effort misdirected are;
And if there's good in war and crime,
There may be in my bits of rhyme,
My song from out the slaughter mill:
So take or leave them as you will.

CONTENTS

CONTENTS

CONTENTS

CONTENTS

CONTENTS

13

CONTENTS

14

THE CALL

(France, August first, 1914.)

Far and near, high and clear,
  Hark to the call of War!
Over the gorse and the golden dells,
Ringing and swinging of clamorous bells,
Praying and saying of wild farewells:
  War! War! War!

High and low, all must go:
  Hark to the shout of War!
Leave to the women the harvest yield;
Gird ye, men, for the sinister field;
A sabre instead of a scythe to wield:
  War! Red War!

Rich and poor, lord and boor,
  Hark to the blast of War!
Tinker and tailor and millionaire,
Actor in triumph and priest in prayer,
Comrades now in the hell out there,—
  Sweep to the fire of War!

15

THE CALL

Prince and page, sot and sage,
    Hark to the roar of War!
Poet, professor and circus clown,
Chimney-sweeper and fop o' the town,
Into the pot and be melted down:
    Into the pot of War!

Women all, hear the call,
    The pitiless call of War!
Look your last on your dearest ones,
Brothers and husbands, fathers, sons:
Swift they go to the ravenous guns,
    The gluttonous guns of War.

Everywhere thrill the air
    The maniac bells of War.
There will be little of sleeping to-night;
There will be wailing and weeping to-night;
Death's red sickle is reaping to-night:
    War! War! War!

THE FOOL

" BUT it isn't playing the game," he said,
　And he slammed his books away;
" The Latin and Greek I've got in my head
　Will do for a duller day."
" Rubbish!" I cried; " The bugle's call
　Isn't for lads from school."
D'ye think he'd listen?　Oh, not at all:
　So I called him a fool, a fool.

Now there's his dog by his empty bed,
　And the flute he used to play,
And his favourite bat—but Dick, he's dead,
　Somewhere in France, they say:
Dick with his rapture of song and sun,
　Dick of the yellow hair,
Dicky whose life had but begun,
　Carrion-cold out there.

2

THE FOOL

Look at his prizes all in a row:
  Surely a hint of fame.
Now he's finished with—nothing to show:
  Doesn't it seem a shame?
Look from the window! All you see
  Was to be his one day:
Forest and furrow, lawn and lea,
  And he goes and chucks it away.

Chucks it away to die in the dark:
  Somebody saw him fall,
Part of him mud, part of him blood,
  The rest of him—not at all.
And yet I'll bet he was never afraid,
  And he went as the best of 'em go;
For his hand was clenched on his broken blade,
  And his face was turned to the foe.

And I called him a fool—oh, blind was I!
  And the cup of my grief's abrim;
Will Glory o' England ever die
  So long as we've lads like him?
So long as we've fond and fearless fools,
  Who, spurning fortune and fame,
Turn out with the rallying cry of their schools,
  Just bent on playing the game.

THE FOOL

A fool! Ah no! He was more than wise,
  His was the proudest part;
He died with the glory of faith in his eyes,
  And the glory of love in his heart.
And though there's never a grave to tell,
  Nor a cross to mark his fall,
Thank God! we know that he " batted well "
  In the last great Game of all.

THE VOLUNTEER

Sez I: My Country calls? Well, let it call.
  I grins perlitely and declines wiv thanks.
Go, let 'em plaster every blighted wall,
  'Ere's *one* they don't stampede into the ranks.
Them politicians with their greasy ways;
  Them empire-grabbers—fight for 'em? No fear!
I've seen this mess a-comin' from the days
  Of Algyserious and Aggydear:
      I've felt me passion rise and swell,
      But—wot the 'ell, Bill? Wot the 'ell?

Sez I: My Country? *Mine?* I likes their cheek:
  Me mud-bespattered by the cars they drive,
Wot makes me measly thirty bob a week,
  And sweats red blood to keep meself alive!
Fight for the right to slave that they may spend,
  Them in their mansions, me 'ere in my slum?
No, let 'em fight wot's something to defend:
  But me, I've nothin';—let the Kaiser come.
      And so I cusses 'ard and well,
      But—wot the 'ell, Bill? Wot the 'ell?

THE VOLUNTEER

Sez I : If they would do the decent thing,
   And shield the missis and the little 'uns,
Why, even *I* might shout " God save the King !"
   And face the chances of them 'ungry guns.
But we've got three, another on the way;
   It's that wot makes me snarl and set me jor :
The wife and nippers, wot of 'em, I say,
   If I gets knocked out in this blasted war?
      Gets proper busted by a shell,
        But—wot the 'ell, Bill? Wot the 'ell?

Ay, wot the 'ell's the use of all this talk?
   To-day some boys in blue was passin' me,
And some of 'em they 'ad no legs to walk,
   And some of 'em they 'ad no eyes to see.
And—well, I couldn't look 'em in the face;
   And so I'm goin', goin' to declare
I'm under forty-one and take me place
   To face the music with the bunch out there.
      A fool, you say! Maybe you're right,
      I'll 'ave no peace unless I fight.
      I've ceased to think; I only know
      I've gotta go, Bill, gotta go.

THE CONVALESCENT

.   .   .   So I walked among the willows very
    quietly all night;
There was no moon at all, at all; no timid star
    alight;
There was no light at all, at all; I wint from tree
    to tree,
And I called him as his mother called, but he
    nivver answered me.

Oh, I called him all the night-time, as I walked
    the wood alone;
And I listened and I listened, but I nivver heard
    a moan;
Then I found him at the dawnin', when the sorry
    sky was red:
I was lookin' for the livin', but I only found the
    dead.

Sure I know that it was Shamus by the silver
    cross he wore;
But the bugles they were callin', and I heard the
    cannon roar.

THE CONVALESCENT

Oh, I had no time to tarry, so I said a little
     prayer
And I clasped his hands together, and I left him
     lyin' there.

Now the birds are singin', singin', and I'm home
     in Donegal,
And it's Springtime, and I'm thinkin' that I only
     dreamed it all;
I dreamed about that evil wood, all crowded
     with its dead,
Where I knelt beside me brother when the battle-
     dawn was red.

Where I prayed beside me brother ere I wint to
     fight anew:
Such dreams as these are evil dreams; I can't
     believe it's true.
Where all is love and laughter, sure it's hard to
     think of loss. . . . . .
But mother's sayin' nothin', and she clasps—*a
silver cross.*

THE MAN FROM ATHABASKA

OH, the wife she tried to tell me that 'twas noth-
   ing but the thrumming
   Of a woodpecker a-rapping on the hollow of a
      tree;
And she thought that I was fooling when I said
      it was the drumming
   Of the mustering of legions, and 'twas calling
      unto me;
   'Twas calling me to pull my freight and hop
      across the sea.

And a-mending of my fish-nets sure I started up
      in wonder,
   For I heard a savage roaring and 'twas coming
      from afar;
Oh, the wife she tried to tell me that 'twas only
      summer thunder,
   And she laughed a bit sarcastic when I told her
      it was war;
   'Twas the chariots of battle where the mighty
      armies are.

THE MAN FROM ATHABASKA

Then down the lake came Half-breed Tom with
   russet sail a-flying,
   And the word he said was " war " again, so
   what was I to do?
Oh, the dogs they took to howling, and the missis
   took to crying,
   As I flung my silver foxes in the little birch
   canoe;
   Yes, the old girl stood a-blubbing till an island
   hid the view.

Says the factor : " Mike, you're crazy ! They have
   soldier-men a-plenty.
   You're as grizzled as a badger, and you're sixty
   year or so."
" But I haven't missed a scrap," says I, " since I
   was one and twenty.
   And shall I miss the biggest? You can bet your
   whiskers—no !"
   So I sold my furs and started . . . . .
   and that's eighteen months ago.

For I joined the Foreign Legion, and they put
   me for a starter
   In the trenches of the Argonne with the Boche
   a step away;

THE MAN FROM ATHABASKA

And the partner on my right hand was an apache
    from Montmartre;
  On my left there was a millionaire from Pitts-
    burg, U.S.A.
  (Poor fellow! They collected him in bits the
    other day.)

But I'm sprier than a chipmunk, save a touch of
    the lumbago;
  And they calls me Old Methoosalah, and
    blagues me all the day,
I'm their exhibition sniper, and they work me
    like a Dago,
  And laugh to see me plug a Boche a half a mile
    away.
  Oh, I hold the highest record in the regiment,
    they say.

And at night they gather 'round me, and I tell
    them of my roaming
  In the Country of the Crepuscule beside the
    Frozen Sea;
Where the musk-ox runs unchallenged, and the
    cariboo goes homing,—
  And they sit like little children, just as quiet
    as can be:
  Men of every clime and colour, how they
    hearken unto me!

THE MAN FROM ATHABASKA

And I tell them of the Furland, of the tumpline
and the paddle,
  Of secret rivers loitering, that no one will
  explore;
And I tell them of the ranges, of the pack-strap
and the saddle,
  And they fill their pipes in silence, and their
  eyes beseech for more;
  While above the star-shells fizzle and the high
  explosives roar.

And I tell of lakes fish-haunted, where the big
bull moose are calling,
  And forests still as sepulchres with never trail
  or track;
And valleys packed with purple gloom, and moun-
tain peaks appalling;
  And I tell them of my cabin on the shore at
  Fond du Lac;
  And I find myself a-thinking: Sure I wish that
  I was back.

So I brag of bear and beaver while the batteries
are roaring,
  And the fellows on the firing steps are blazing
  at the foe;

THE MAN FROM ATHABASKA

And I yarn of fur and feather when the *marmites*
    are a-soaring,
  And they listen to my stories, seven *poilus* in
    a row,
  Seven lean and lousy *poilus* with their cigar-
    ettes aglow.

And I tell them when it's over how I'll hike for
    Athabaska;
  And those seven greasy *poilus* they are crazy
    to go too.
And I'll give the wife the " pickle-tub " I pro-
    mised and I'll ask her
  The price of mink and marten, and the run of
    cariboo;
  And I'll get my traps in order, and I'll start to
    work anew.

For I've had my fill of fighting, and I've seen a
    nation scattered;
  And an army swung to slaughter, and a river
    red with gore;
And a city all a-smoulder, and . . . as if it
    really mattered,
  For the lake is yonder dreaming, and my
    cabin's on the shore;
And the dogs are leaping madly, and the wife is
    singing gladly,
  And I'll rest in Athabaska, and I'll leave it
    never more.

THE RED RETREAT

Tramp, tramp, the grim road, the road from Mons
    to Wipers;
    (I've 'ammered out this ditty with me bruised
     and bleedin' feet;)
Tramp, tramp, the dim road—we didn't 'ave no
    pipers,
    And bellies that was 'oller was the drums we
    'ad to beat.
Tramp, tramp, the bad road, the bits o' kiddies
    cryin' there;
    The fell birds a-flyin' there, the 'ouses all
    aflame;
Tramp, tramp, the sad road, the pals I left a-lyin'
    there,
    Red there, and dead there—Oh blimy, it's a
    shame!

A-singin' "'Oo's Yer Lady Friend?" we started
    out from 'Arver,
    A-singin' till our froats was dry—we didn't
    care a 'ang;

THE RED RETREAT

The Frenchies 'ow they lined the way, and slung
    us their palaver,
  And all we knowed to arnser was the one word
    " vang ";
They gave us booze and caporal, and cheered for
    us like crazy,
  And all the pretty gels was out to kiss us as
    we passed;
And 'ow they all went dotty when we 'owled the
    Marcelaisey!
  Oh Gawd! Them was the 'appy days, the days
    too good to last.

We started out fro' God Knows Where, we
    started out a-roarin';
  We 'ollered: " 'Ere We Are Again," and
    'struth! but we was dry.
The dust was gummin' up our ears, and 'ow the
    sweat was pourin'!
  The road was long, the sun was like a brazier
    in the sky.
We wondered where the 'Uns was—we wasn't
    long a-wonderin'!
  For down a scruff of 'ill-side they rushes like
    a flood;

THE RED RETREAT

Then, oh! 'twas music 'eavenly, our batteries
a-thunderin',
And arms and legs went soarin' in the fountain
of their blood.

For on they came like bee-swarms a-hochin' and
a-singin';
We pumped the bullets into 'em, we couldn't
miss a shot.
But though we mowed 'em down like grass, like
grass was they a-springin',
And all our 'ands was blistered, for our rifles
was so 'ot.
We roared with battle-fury, and we lammed the
stuffin' out of 'em,
And then we fixed our bay'nets and we spitted
'em like meat.
You should 'ave 'eard the beggars squeal; you
should 'ave seen the rout of 'em,
And 'ow we cussed and wondered when the
word came: Retreat.

Retreat! That was the 'ell of it. It fair upset
our 'abits,
A-runnin' from them blighters over 'alf the
roads of France;

THE RED RETREAT

A-scurryin' before 'em like a lot of blurry rabbits,
　　And knowin' we could smash 'em if we just 'ad
　　　'alf a chance.
Retreat! That was the bitter bit, a-limpin' and
　　a-blunderin';
　　All day and night a-hoofin' it and sleepin' on
　　　our feet;
A-fightin' rear-guard actions for a bit o' rest, and
　　wonderin'
　　If sugar beets or mangels was the 'olesomest to
　　　eat.

Ho yus! there isn't many left that started out so
　　cheerily!
　　There was no bands a-playin' and we 'ad no
　　　autmobeels.
Our tummies they was 'oller, and our 'eads was
　　'angin' wearily,
　　And if we stopped to light a fag the 'Uns was
　　　on our 'eels.
That rotten road! I can't forget the kids and
　　mothers flyin' there;
　　The bits of barns a-blazin' and the 'orrid sights
　　　I sor;
The stiffs that lined the wayside, me own pals
　　a-lyin' there,
　　Their faces covered over wiv a little 'eap of
　　　stror.

THE RED RETREAT

Tramp, tramp, the red road, the wicked bullets
    'ummin',
    (I've panted out this ditty with me 'ot 'ard
      breath.)
Tramp, tramp, the dread road, the Boches all
    a-comin',
    The lootin' and the shootin' and the shrieks o'
      death.
Tramp, tramp, the fell road, the mad 'orde pur-
    suin' there,
    And 'ow we 'urled it back again, them grim,
      grey waves;
    Tramp, tramp, the 'ell road, the 'orror and the
      ruin there,
    The graves of me mateys there, the grim, sour
      graves.

THE HAGGIS OF PRIVATE McPHEE

" HA'E ye heard whit ma auld mither's postit tae
    me?
It fair mak's me hamesick," says Private McPhee.
" And whit did she send ye?" says Private
    McPhun,
As he cockit his rifle and bleezed at a Hun,
" A haggis! *A haggis!*" says Private McPhee;
" The brawest big haggis I ever did see.
And think! it's the morn when fond memory
    turns
Tae haggis and whuskey—the birthday o' Burns.
We maun find a dram; then we'll ca' in the rest
O' the lads, and we'll ha'e a Burns' nicht wi' the
    best."

" Be ready at sundoon," snapped Sergeant Mc-
    Cole;
" I want you two men for the list'nin' patrol."
Then Private McPhee looked at Private McPhun;
" I'm thinkin', ma lad, we're confoundedly done."

THE HAGGIS OF PRIVATE McPHEE

Then Private McPhun looked at Private McPhee:
" I'm thinkin', auld chap, it's a' aff wi' oor spree."
But up spoke their crony, wee Wullie McNair:
" Jist lea' yer braw haggis for me tae prepare;
And as for the dram, if I search the camp roun',
We maun ha'e a drappie tae jist haud it doon.
Sae rin, lads, and think, though the nicht it be
  black,
O' the haggis that's waitin' ye when ye get back."

My! but it wis waesome on Naebuddy's Land,
And the deid they were rottin' on every hand,
And the rockets like corpse candles hauntit the
  sky;
And the winds o' destruction went shudderin' by.
There wis skelpin' o' bullets and skirlin' o' shells,
And breengin' o' bombs and a thousand death-
  knells;
But cooryin' doon in a Jack Johnson hole
Little fashed the twa men o' the list'nin' patrol.
For sweeter than honey and bricht as a gem
Wis the thocht o' the haggis that waitit for them.

Yet alas! in oor moments o' sunniest cheer
Calamity's aften maist cruelly near;
And while the twa talked o' their puddin' divine,
The Boches below them were howkin' a mine.

35

THE HAGGIS OF PRIVATE McPHEE

And while the twa cracked o' the feast they would
    ha'e,
The fuse it wis burnin' and burnin' away;
Then sudden a roar like the thunner o' doom,
A hell-leap o' flame . . . . . then the wheesht
    o' the tomb.

" Haw Jock! Are ye hurtit?" says Private
    McPhun.
" Ay, Geordie, they've got me; I'm fearin' I'm
    done.
It's ma leg; I'm jist thinkin' it's aff at the knee;
Ye'd best gang and leave me," says Private
    McPhee.
" Oh leave ye I wunna," says Private McPhun;
" And leave ye I canna, for though I micht run,
It's no faur I wud gang, it's no muckle I'd see;
I'm blindit, and that's whit's the maitter wi' me."
Then Private McPhee sadly shakit his heid:
" If we bide here for lang, we'll be bidin' for deid.
And yet, Geordie lad, I could gang weel content
If I'd tasted that haggis ma auld mither sent."
" That's droll," says McPhun; " ye've jist speakit
    ma mind.
Oh, I ken it's a terrible thing tae be blind;
And yet it's no' that that embitters ma lot—
It's missin' that braw muckle haggis ye've got."

THE HAGGIS OF PRIVATE McPHEE

For a while they were silent; then up once again
Spoke Private McPhee, though he whussilt wi'
    pain:
" And why should we miss it?   Between you and
    me
We've legs for tae run, and we've eyes for tae see.
You lend me your shanks and I'll lend you ma
    sicht,
And we'll baith ha'e a kyte-fu' o' haggis the
    nicht."

Oh! the sky it wis dourlike and dreepin' a wee,
When Private McPhun gruppit Private McPhee.
Oh! the glaur it wis fylin' and crieshin' the grun,
When Private McPhee guidit Private McPhun.
" Keep clear o' them corpses—they're maybe no
    deid!
Haud on! there's a big muckle crater aheid.
Look oot! There's a sap; we'll be haein' a coup.
A staur-shell! for Godsake! Doon, lad, on yer
    daup.
Bear aff tae yer richt. . . . . Aw yer jist
    daein' fine:
Before the nicht's feenished on haggis we'll dine "

There wis death and destruction on every hand;
There wis havoc and horror on Naebuddy's
    Land;

THE HAGGIS OF PRIVATE McPHEE

And the shells bickered doon wi' a crump and a
      glare,
And the hameless wee bullets were dingin' the
      air.
Yet on they went staggerin', cooryin' doon
When the stutter and cluck o' a Maxim crept
      roun'.
And the legs o' McPhun they were sturdy and
      stoot,
And McPhee on his back kept a bonnie look-out.
" On, on, ma brave lad! We're no' faur frae the
      goal;
I can hear the braw sweerin' o' Sergeant McCole."

But strength has its leemit, and Private McPhun,
Wi' a sab and a curse fell his length on the grun.
Then Private McPhee shoutit doon in his ear:
" Jist think o' the haggis! I smell it from here.
It's gushin' wi' juice, it's embaumin' the air;
It's steamin' for us, and we're jist—aboot—
      there."
Then Private McPhee answers: " Dammit, auld
      chap!
For the sake o' that haggis I'll gang till I drap."
And he gets on his feet wi' a heave and a strain,
And onward he staggers in passion and pain.

THE HAGGIS OF PRIVATE McPHEE

And the flare and the glare and the fury increase,
Till you'd think they'd jist taken a' hell on a
     lease.
And on they go reelin' in peetiful plight,
And someone is shoutin' away on their right;
And someone is running; and noo they can hear
A sound like a prayer and a sound like a cheer;
And swift through the crash and the flash and
     the din,
The lads o' the Hielands are bringin' them in.

" They're baith sairly woundit, but is it no droll
Hoo they rave aboot haggis?" says Sergeant
     McCole,
When hirplin' alang comes wee Wullie McNair,
And they a' wonert why he wis greetin' sae sair.
And he says: " I'd jist liftit it oot o' the pot,
And there it lay steamin' and savoury hot;
When sudden I dooked at the fleech o' a shell,
And it—*drapped on the haggis and dinged it tae
     hell.*"

And oh! but the lads were fair taken aback,
Then sudden the order wis passed tae attack.
And up from the trenches like lions they leapt,

THE HAGGIS OF PRIVATE McPHEE

And on through the nicht like a torrent they
    swept.
On, on, wi' their bayonets thirstin' before!
On, on tae the foe wi' a rush and a roar!
And wild to the welkin their battle-cry rang,
And doon on the Boches like tigers they sprang;
And there wisna' a man but had death in his ee,
For he thocht o' the haggis o' Private McPhee.

THE LARK

From wrath-red dawn to wrath-red dawn,
  The guns have brayed without abate;
And now the sick sun looks upon
  The bleared, blood-boltered fields of hate
As if it loathed to rise again.
  How strange the hush! Yet sudden, hark!
From yon down-trodden gold of grain,
  The leaping rapture of a lark.

A fusillade of melody,
  That sprays us from yon trench of sky;
A new amazing enemy
  We cannot silence though we try;
A battery on radiant wings,
  That from yon gap of golden fleece
Hurls at us hopes of such strange things
  As joy and home and love and peace.

THE LARK

Pure heart of song! do you not know
  That we are making earth a hell?
Or is it that you try to show
  Life still is joy and all is well?
Brave little wings! Ah, not in vain
  You beat into that bit of blue:
Lo! we who pant in war's red rain
  Lift shining eyes, see Heaven too.

THE ODYSSEY OF 'ERBERT 'IGGINS

ME and Ed and a stretcher
   Out on the nootral ground.
(If there's one dead corpse, I'll betcher
   There's a 'undred smellin' around.)
Me and Eddie O'Brian,
   Both of the R.A.M.C.
(" It's a 'ell of a night
For a soul to take flight,"
   As Eddie remarks to me.)
Me and Ed crawlin' 'omeward,
   Thinkin' our job is done,
When sudden and clear,
Wot do we 'ear?
   'Owl of a wounded 'Un.

"Got to take 'im," snaps Eddy;
   "Got to take all we can;
'E may be a Germ.
Wiv the 'eart of a worm,
   But, blarst 'im! ain't 'e a man?"
So 'e sloshes out fixin' a dressin',
   ('E'd always a medical knack),

43

THE ODYSSEY OF 'ERBERT 'IGGINS

When that wounded 'Un
'E rolls to 'is gun,
    And 'e plugs me pal in the back.

Now what would you do, I arst you?
    There was me slaughtered mate.
There was that 'Un
(I'd collared 'is gun),
    A-snarlin' 'is 'ymn of 'ate.
Wot did I do? 'Ere, whisper. . . . .
    'E'd a shiny bald top to 'is 'ead;
But when I got through,
Between me and you,
    It was 'orrid and jaggy and red.

" 'Ang on like a limpet, Eddy.
    Thank Gord! you ain't dead after all."
It's slow and it's sure and it's steady,
    (Which is 'ard, for 'e's big and I'm small.)
The rockets are shootin' and shinin'.
    It's rainin' a perishin' flood,
The bullets are buzzin' and whinin',
    And I'm up to me stern in the mud.
There's all kinds of 'owlin' and 'ootin';
    It's black as a bucket of tar;
Oh! I'm doin' my bit,
But I'm 'avin' a fit,
    And I wish I was 'ome wiv Mar.

THE ODYSSEY OF 'ERBERT 'IGGINS

"Stick on like a plaster, Eddy.
  Old sport, you're a-slakin' your grip."
Gord! But I'm crocky already;
  My feet, 'ow they slither and slip!
There goes the biff of a bullet.
  The Boches have got us for fair.
Another one—*Whut!*
The son of a slut!
  'E managed to miss by a 'air.
'Ow! Wot was it jabbed at me shoulder?
  Gave it a dooce of a wrench.
Is it Eddy or me
Wot's a-bleedin' so free?
  Crust! but it's long to the trench.
I ain't just as strong as a Sandow,
  And Ed ain't a flapper by far;
I'm blamed if I understand 'ow
  We've managed to get where we are.
But 'ere's for a bit of a breather.
  "Steady there, Ed, 'arf a mo'.
Old pal, it's all right;
It's a 'ell of a fight,
  But are we down'earted? No—o—o."

Now war is a funny thing, ain't it?
  It's the rummiest sort of a go.

THE ODYSSEY OF 'ERBERT 'IGGINS

For when it's most real,
It's then that you feel
    You're a-watchin' a cinema show.
'Ere's me wot's a barber's assistant,
    Hey, presto! It's somewheres in France,
And I'm 'ere in a pit
Where a coal-box 'as 'it,
    And it's all like a giddy romance.
The ruddy quick-firers are spittin',
    The 'eavies are bellowin' 'ate,
And 'ere I am cashooly sittin',
    And 'oldin' the 'ead of me mate.
Them gharstly green star-shells is beamin',
    'Ot shrapnel is poppin' like rain,
And I'm sayin': " Bert 'Iggins, you're dreamin',
    And you'll wake up in 'Ampstead again.
You'll wake up and 'ear yourself sayin':
    ' Would you like, sir, to 'ave a shampoo?'
'Stead of sheddin' yer blood
In the rain and the mud,
    Which is somehow the right thing to do;
Which is some'ow yer 'oary-eyed dooty,
    Wot you're doin' the best wot you can,
For 'Ampstead and 'ome and beauty,
    And you've been and you've slaughtered a
        man,

46

THE ODYSSEY OF 'ERBERT 'IGGINS

A feller wot punctured your partner;
   Oh, you 'ammered 'im 'ard on the 'ead,
And you still see 'is eyes
Starin' bang at the skies,
   And you ain't even sorry 'e's dead.
But you wish you was back in your diggin's,
   Asleep on your mouldy old stror.
Oh! you're doin' yer bit, 'Erbert 'Iggins,
   But you ain't just enjoyin' the war."

'Ang on like a hoctopus, Eddy.
   It's us for the bomb-belt again.
Except for the shrap.
Which 'as 'it me a tap,
   I'm feelin' as right as the rain.
It's my silly old feet wot are slippin',
   It's as dark as a 'ogs'ead o' sin,
But don't be oneasy, my pippin,
   I'm goin' to pilot you in.
It's my silly old 'ead wot is reelin'.
   The bullets is buzzin' like bees.
Me shoulder's red-'ot,
And I'm bleedin' a lot,
   And me legs is on'inged at the knees.
But we're staggerin' nearer and nearer,
   Just stick it, old sport, play the game.

THE ODYSSEY OF 'ERBERT 'IGGINS

I make 'em out clearer and clearer,
  Our trenches a-snappin' with flame.
Oh! we're stumblin' closer and closer.
  'Ang on there, lad! Just one more try.
Did you say: Put you down? Damn it, no, sir!
  I'll carry you in if I die.
By cracky! old feller, they've seen us,
  They're sendin' out stretchers for two;
Let's give 'em the hoorah between us,
  ('Anged lucky we aren't booked through.)
My flipper is mashed to a jelly.
  A bullet 'as tickled your spleen.
We've shed lots of gore
And we're leakin' some more,
  But—wot a hoccasion it's been!
Ho! 'Ere comes the rescuin' party.
  They're crawlin' out cautious and slow.
Come! Buck up and greet 'em, my 'earty,
  Shoulder to shoulder,—so.
They must'nt think we was down'earted.
Old pal, we was never down'earted;
If they arsts us if we was down'earted
  We'll 'owl in their fyces—No—o—o.

A SONG OF WINTER WEATHER

IT isn't the foe that we fear;
  It isn't the bullets that whine;
It isn't the business career
  Of a shell, or the bust of a mine.
It isn't the snipers who seek
  To nip our young hopes in the bud:
No, it isn't the guns,
And it isn't the Huns,—
  It's the MUD,
          MUD,
                  MUD.

It isn't the *mêlée* we mind.
  That often is rather good fun.
It isn't the shrapnel we find
  Obtrusive when rained by the ton.
It isn't the bounce of the bombs
  That gives us a positive pain:
It's the strafing we get
When the weather is wet,—
  It's the RAIN,
          RAIN,
                  RAIN

A SONG OF WINTER WEATHER

It isn't because we lack grit
  We shrink from the horrors of war.
We don't mind the battle a bit;
  In fact that is what we are for.
It isn't the rum-jars and things
  Make us wish we were back in the fold:
It's the fingers that freeze
In the boreal breeze,—
  It's the COLD,
          COLD,
              COLD.

Oh the rain, the mud and the cold,
  The cold, the mud and the rain;
With weather at zero it's hard for a hero
  From language that's rude to refrain.
With porridgy muck to the knees,
  With sky that's a-pouring a flood,
Sure the worst of our foes
Are the pains and the woes
  Of the RAIN,
          THE COLD,
              AND THE MUD.

TIPPERARY DAYS

Oh weren't they the fine boys! You never saw
    the beat of them,
  Singing all together with their throats bronze-
    bare;
Fighting-fit and mirth-mad, music in the feet of
    them,
  Swinging on to glory and the wrath out there.
Laughing by and chaffing by, frolic in the smiles
    of them,
  On the road, the white road, all the afternoon;
Strangers in a strange land, miles and miles and
    miles of them,
  Battle-bound and heart-high, and singing this
    tune:—
      It's a long way to Tipperary,
        It's a long way to go;
      It's a long way to Tipperary,
        And the sweetest girl I know.
      Good-bye Piccadilly,
        Farewell Lester Square:
      It's a long, long way to Tipperary,
        But my heart's right there.

TIPPERARY DAYS

"Come Yvonne and Juliette! Come Mimi and
 cheer for them!
  Throw them flowers and kisses as they pass
  you by.
 Aren't they the lovely lads! Haven't you a
  tear for them
  Going out so gallantly to dare and die?
What is it they're singing so? Some high hymn
 of Motherland?
  Some immortal chanson of their Faith and
  King?
Marseillaise or Brabançon, anthem of that
 other land,—
  Dears, let us remember it, that song they
  sing:—

 "*C'est un chemin long* ' *to Tepararee,*'
 C'est un chemin long, c'est vrai;
 C'est un chemin long ' *to Tepararee,*'
 Et la belle fille qu'je connais.
 Bonjour, Peekadeely!
 Au revoir, Lestaire Square!
 C'est un chemin long ' *to Tepararee,*'
 Mais mon coeur ' *ees zaire.*' "

TIPPERARY DAYS

The gallant old " Contemptibles!" There isn't
   much remains of them,
  So full of fun and fitness, and a-singing in their
    pride;
For some are cold as clabber and the corby picks
   the brains of them,
  And some are back in Blighty, and a-wishing
    they had died.
Ah me! It seems but yesterday, that great, glad
   sight of them,
  Swinging on to battle as the sky grew black
    and black;
Yet Oh! their glee and glory, and the great, grim
   fight of them!
  Just whistle Tipperary and it all comes back:
    It's a long way to Tipperary,
      (*Which means " 'ome " anywhere;*)
    It's a long way to Tipperary,
      (*And the things wot make you care.*)
    Good-bye Piccadilly,
      (*'Ow I 'opes my folks is well!*)
    It's a long, long way to Tipperary—
      (*'R! Ain't War just 'ell?*)

FLEURETTE

(The Wounded Canadian Speaks).

My leg? It's off at the knee.
Do I miss it? Well, some. You see
  I've had it since I was born;
  And, lately, a devilish corn.
(I rather chuckle with glee
  To think how I've fooled that corn.)

But I'll hobble around all right.
  It isn't that, it's my face.
Oh I know I'm a hideous sight,—
  Hardly a thing in place.
Sort of gargoyle, you'd say.
  Nurse won't give me a glass;
  But I see the folks as they pass
Shudder and turn away;
  Turn away in distress. . . . .
  Mirror enough, I guess.

FLEURETTE

I'm gay! You bet I *am* gay;
  But I wasn't a while ago;
If you'd seen me even to-day,
  The darndest picture of woe,
With this Caliban mug of mine,
  So ravaged and raw and red,
Turned to the wall,—in fine
  Wishing that I was dead. . . . .
What has happened since then?
  Since I lay with face to the wall,
The most despairing of men:
  Listen! I'll tell you all.

That *poilu* across the way,
  With the shrapnel wound in his head,
Has a sister; she came to-day
  To sit awhile by his bed.
All morning I heard him fret:
" Oh, when will she come, Fleurette?"

Then sudden a joyous cry,
  The tripping of little feet,
The softest, tenderest sigh,
  A voice so fresh and sweet;

FLEURETTE

Clear as a silver bell;
　　Fresh as the morning dews:
" *C'est toi, c'est toi, Marcel!*
　　Mon frère, comme je suis heureuse!"

So over the blanket's rim
　　I raised my terrible face,
And I saw (how I envied him!)
　　A girl of such delicate grace;
Sixteen, all laughter and love;
　　As gay as a linnet, and yet
As tenderly sweet as a dove,
　　Half woman, half child,—Fleurette.

Then I turned to the wall again,
　　(I was awfully blue, you see,)
And I thought with a bitter pain:
　　" Such visions are not for me."
So there like a log I lay,
　　All hidden, I thought, from view,
When sudden I heard her say:
　　" Ah! Who is that *malheureux?*"
Then briefly I heard him tell
　　(However he came to know)
How I'd smothered a bomb that fell
　　Into the trench, and so
None of my men were hit,
Though it busted me up a bit.

56

FLEURETTE

Well, I didn't quiver an eye,
    And he chattered, and there she sat;
And I fancied I heard her sigh,
    Though I wouldn't just swear to that.
And maybe she wasn't so bright,
    Though she talked in a merry strain;
And I closed my eyes ever so tight,
    Yet I saw her ever so plain;
Her dear little tilted nose,
    Her delicate, dimpled chin,
Her mouth like a budding rose,
    And the glistening pearls within;
Her eyes like the violet,
Such a rare little queen—Fleurette!

And at last when she rose to go,
    The light was a little dim,
And I ventures to peep, and so
    I saw her, graceful and slim;
And she kissed him and kissed him, and Oh!
    How I envied and envied him!

So when she was gone I said
    In rather a dreary voice
To him of the opposite bed:
    " Ah, friend! how you must rejoice!

FLEURETTE

But me, I'm a thing of dread,
   For me nevermore the bliss,
   The thrill of a woman's kiss."

Then I stopped, for lo! she was there,
   And a great light shone in her eyes;
And me, I could only stare,
   I was taken so by surprise,
When gently she bent her head:
"May I kiss you, sergeant?" she said.

Then she kissed my burning lips,
   With her mouth like a scented flower;
And I thrilled to the finger-tips,
   And I hadn't even the power
To say: "God bless you, dear;"
And I felt such a precious tear
   Fall on my withered cheek,
   And darn it! I couldn't speak.

And so she went sadly away,
   And I knew that my eyes were wet;
Ah! not to my dying day
   Will I forget, forget.
Can you wonder now I am gay?
   God bless her, that little Fleurette!

FUNK

When your marrer bones seems 'oller,
And you're glad you ain't no taller,
   And you're all a-shakin' like you 'ad the chills;
When your skin creeps like a pullet's,
And you're duckin' all the bullets,
   And you're green as gorgonzola round the gills;
When your legs seem made of jelly,
And you're squeamish in the belly,
   And you wants to turn about and do a bunk:
For Gawd's sake, kid, don't show it!
Don't let your mateys know it,—
   You're just sufferin' from funk, funk, funk.

Of course there's no denyin'
That it ain't so easy tryin'
   To grin and grip your rifle by the butt,
When the 'ole world rips asunder,
And you sees yer pal go under,
   As a bunch of shrapnel sprays 'im on the nut;

FUNK

I admit it's 'ard contrivin'
When you 'ears the shells arrivin',
   To discover you're a bloomin' bit o' spunk;
But, my lad, you've got to do it,
And your God will see you through it,
   For wot 'e 'ates is funk, funk, funk.

So stand up, son; look gritty,
And just 'um a lively ditty,
   And only be afraid to be afraid;
Just 'old yer rifle steady,
And 'ave yer bay'nit ready,
   For that's the way good soldier-men is made.
And if you 'as to die,
As it sometimes 'appens, why,
   Far better die a 'ero than a skunk,
A-doin' of yer bit,
And so—to 'ell with it,
   There ain't no bloomin' funk, funk, funk.

OUR HERO

" Flowers, only flowers,—bring me dainty posies,
  Blossoms for forgetfulness," that was all he
    said;
So we sacked our gardens, violets and roses,
  Lilies white and blue-bells laid we on his bed.
Soft his pale hands touched them, tenderly
    caressing;
  Soft into his tired eyes came a little light;
Such a wistful love-look, gentle as a blessing;
  There amid the flowers waited he the night.

" I would have you raise me; I can see the West
    then:
  I would see the sun set once before I go."
So he lay a-gazing, seemed to be at rest then,
  Quiet as a spirit in the golden glow.
So he lay a-watching rosy castles crumbling,
  Moats of blinding amber, bastions of flame,
Rugged rifts of opal, crimson turrets tumbling;
  So he lay a-dreaming till the shadows came.

OUR HERO

" Open wide the window; there's a lark a-singing;
   There's a glad lark singing in the evening sky.
How it's wild with rapture, radiantly winging!
   Oh it's good to hear that when one has to die!
I am horror-haunted from the hell they found
      me;
   I am battle-broken, all I want is rest.
Ah! It's good to die so, blossoms all around me,
   And a kind lark singing in the golden West."

" Flowers, song and sunshine, just one thing is
      wanting,
   Just the happy laughter of a little child."
So we brought our dearest, Doris all-enchanting;
   Tenderly he kissed her; radiant he smiled.
" In the golden peace-time you will tell the story
   How for you and yours, sweet, bitter deaths
      were ours.   .   .   .
God bless little children!" So he passed to glory,
   So we left him sleeping, still amid the flow'rs.

MY MATE

I'VE been sittin' starin', starin' at 'is muddy pair
    of boots,
  An tryin' to convince meself it's 'im.
(Look out there, lad! That sniper,—'e's a dysey
    wen 'e shoots;
  'E'll be layin' of you out the same as Jim.)
Jim as lies there in the dug-out wiv 'is blanket
    round 'is 'ead,
  To keep 'is brains from mixin' wiv the mud;
And 'is face as white as putty, and his overcoat
    all red,
  Like 'e's spilt a bloomin' paint-pot,—but it's
    blood.

And I'm tryin' to remember of a time we wasn't
    pals.
  'Ow often we've played 'ookey, 'im and me;
And sometimes it was music-'alls, and sometimes
    it was gals,
  And even there we 'ad no disagree.

MY MATE

For when 'e copped Maria Jones, the one I liked
      the best,
  I shook 'is 'and and loaned 'im 'arf a quid;
I saw 'im through the parson's job, I 'elped 'im
      make 'is nest,
  I even stood god-father to the kid.

So when the war broke out, sez 'e: " Well, wot
      abaht it, Joe?"
  " Well, wot abaht it, lad?" sez I to 'im.
'Is missis made a awful fuss, but 'e was mad
      to go,
  ('E always was 'igh-sperrited was Jim.)
Well, none of it's been 'eaven, and the most of
      it's been 'ell,
  But we've shared our baccy, and we've 'alved
      our bread.
We'd all the luck at Wipers, and we shaved
      through Noove Chapelle,
  And . . . . that snipin' barstard gits 'im
      on the 'ead.

Now wot I wants to know is—why it wasn't me
      was took?
  I've only got meself, 'e stands for three.

MY MATE

I'm plainer than a louse, while 'e was 'andsome
as a dook;
'E always *was* a better man than me.
'E was goin' 'ome next Toosday; 'e was 'appy as
a lark,
And 'e'd just received a letter from his kid;
And 'e struck a match to show me, as we stood
there in the dark,
When . . . .   that bleedin' bullet got 'im
on the lid.

'E was killed so awful sudden that 'e 'adn't time
to die.
'E sorto jumped, and came down wiv a thud.
Them corpsy-lookin' star-shells kept a-streamin'
in the sky,
And there 'e lay like nothin' in the mud.
And there 'e lay so quiet wiv no mansard to 'is
'ead,
And I'm sick, and blamed if I can understand:
The pots of 'alf and 'alf we've 'ad, and *zip!* like
that—'e's dead,
Wiv the letter of 'is nipper in 'is 'and.

There's some as fights for freedom and there's
some as fights for fun,
But me, my lad, I fights for bleedin' 'ate.

5   65

MY MATE

You can blame the war and blast it, but I 'opes
    it won't be done
  Till I gets the bloomin' blood-price for me
    mate.
It'll take a bit o' bayonet to level up for Jim;
    Then if I'm spared I think I'll 'ave a bid,
Wiv 'er that was Mariar Jones to take the place
    of 'im,
    To sorter be a farther to 'is kid.

MILKING TIME

THERE'S a drip of honeysuckle in the deep green
    lane;
There's old Martin jogging homeward on his
    worn old wain;
There are cherry petals falling, and a cuckoo
    calling, calling,
And a score of larks (God bless 'em) . . . .
    but it's all pain, pain.
For you see I am not really there at all, not at
    all;
For you see I'm in the trenches where the crump-
    crumps fall;
And the bits o' shells are screaming and it's only
    blessèd dreaming
That in fancy I am seeming back in old Saint
    Pol.

Oh! I've thought of it so often since I've come
    down here;
And I never dreamt that any place could be so
    dear;

MILKING TIME

The silvered whinstone houses, and the rosy men
    in blouses,
And the kindly, white-capped women with their
    eyes spring-clear.
And mother's sitting knitting where her roses
    climb,
And the angelus is calling with a soft, soft chime,
And the sea-wind comes caressing, and the light's
    a golden blessing,
And Yvonne, Yvonne is guessing that it's milk-
    ing time.
Oh! it's Sunday, for she's wearing of her 'broid-
    ered gown;
And she draws the pasture pickets and the cows
    come down;
And their feet are powdered yellow, and their
    voices honey-mellow,
And they bring a scent of clover, and their eyes
    are brown.
And Yvonne is dreaming after, but her eyes are
    blue;
And her lips are made for laughter, and her
    white teeth, too;
And her mouth is like a cherry, and a dimple
    mocking merry
Is lurking in the very cheek she turns to you.

MILKING TIME

So I walk beside her kindly, and she laughs at
    me;
And I heap her arms with lilac from the lilac
    tree;
And a golden light is welling, and a golden peace
    is dwelling,
And a thousand birds are telling how it's good
    to be.
And what are pouting lips for if they can't be
    kissed?
And I've filled her arms with blossom so she can't
    resist;
And the cows are sadly straying, and her mother
    must be saying
That Yvonne is long delaying. . . . *God!*
    How close that missed.

A nice polite reminder that the Boche are nigh;
That we're here to fight like devils, and if need
    be die;
That from kissing pretty wenches to the frantic
    firing-benches
Of the battered, tattered trenches is a far, far
    cry.

MILKING TIME

Yet still I'm sitting dreaming in the glare and
    grime,
And once again I'm hearing of them church bells
    chime;
And how I wonder whether in the golden summer
    weather
We will fetch the cows together when it's milk-
    ing time! . . .

English voice, months later:

" Ow, Bill! A rottin' Frenchy. Whew! 'E ain't
    'arf prime."

YOUNG FELLOW MY LAD

" WHERE are you going, young fellow my lad,
    On this glittering morn of May?"
" I'm going to join the colours, dad;
    They're looking for men, they say."
" But you're only a boy, young fellow my lad;
    You aren't obliged to go."
" I'm seventeen and a quarter, dad,
    And ever so strong, you know."

*   *   *   *   *   *   *   *   *   *

" So you're off to France, young fellow my lad,
    And you're looking so fit and bright."
" I'm terribly sorry to leave you, dad,
    But I feel that I'm doing right."
" God bless you and keep you, young fellow my
        lad,
    You're all of my life, you know."
" Don't worry. I'll soon be back, dear dad,
    And I'm awfully proud to go."

*   *   *   *   *   *   *   *   *   *

" Why don't you write, young fellow my lad?
    I watch for the post each day;

YOUNG FELLOW MY LAD

And I miss you so, and I'm awfully sad,
    And it's months since you went away.
And I've had the fire in the parlour lit,
    And I'm keeping it burning bright
Till my boy comes home; and here I sit
    Into the quiet night."

*   *   *   *   *   *   *   *   *   *

" What is the matter, young fellow my lad?
    No letter again to-day.
Why did the postman look so sad,
    And sigh as he turned away?
I hear them tell that we've gained new ground,
    But a terrible price we've paid.
God grant, my boy, that you're safe and sound;
    But Oh! I'm afraid, afraid."

*   *   *   *   *   *   *   *   *   *

" They've told me the truth, young fellow my lad:
    You'll never come back again;
  (*Oh God! the dreams and the dreams I've had,*
    And the hopes I've nursed in vain!)
For you passed in the night, young fellow my
    lad,
    And you proved in the cruel test
Of the screaming shell and the battle-hell
    That my boy was one of the best."

YOUNG FELLOW MY LAD

" So you'll live, you'll live, young fellow my lad,
   In the gleam of the evening star,
In the wood note wild and the laugh of the child,
   In all sweet things that are.
And you'll never die, my wonderful boy,
   While life is noble and true,
For all our beauty and peace and joy
   We will owe to our lads like you."

A SONG OF THE SANDBAGS

No, Bill, I'm not a-spooning out no patriotic
   tosh,
  (The cove behind the sandbags ain't a death-
    or-glory cuss) ;
And though I strafes 'em good and 'ard I doesn't
   'ate the Boche,—
  I guess they're mostly decent, just the same as
    most of us.
I guess they loves their 'omes and kids as much
   as you or me,
  And just the same as you or me they'd rather
    shake than fight;
And if we'd 'appened to be born at Berlin-on-
   the-Spree,
  We'd be out there with 'Ans and Fritz, dead
    sure that we was right.

   A-standin' up to the sandbags
    It's funny the thoughts wot come;
   Starin' into the darkness,
    'Earin' the bullets 'um;

74

A SONG OF THE SANDBAGS

(*Zing! Zip! Ping! Rip!*
'Ark 'ow the bullets 'um!)
A-leanin' against the sandbags
    Wiv me rifle under me ear,
  Oh! I've 'ad more thoughts on a sentry-go
    Than I used to 'ave in a year.

I wonder, Bill, if 'Ans and Fritz is wonderin'
    like me
  Wot's at the bottom of it all? Wot all the
    slaughter's for?
'E thinks 'e's right (of course 'e ain't), but this
    we both agree,
  If them as made it 'ad to fight there wouldn't
    be no war.
If them as lies in feather beds while we kips in
    the mud,
  If them as makes their fortoons while we fights
    for 'em like 'ell,
If them as slings their pots of ink just 'ad to
    sling their blood:
  By Crust! I'm thinkin' there'd be another tale
    to tell.

Shiverin' up to the sandbags,
    With a hicicle 'stead of a spine,
  Don't it seem funny the things you think
    'Ere in the firin' line:

A SONG OF THE SANDBAGS

(*Wee! Whut! Ziz! Zut!*
  Lord! 'Ow the bullets whine!)
Hunkerin' down when a star-shell
  Cracks in a sputter of light,
You can jaw to yer soul by the sandbags
  Most any old time o' night.

They talks of England's glory and a-'oldin' of our
    trade.
  Of Empire and 'igh destiny until we're fair
    flim-flammed;
But if it's for the likes o' that that bloody war is
    made,
  Then wot I say is: Empire and 'igh destiny be
    damned!
There's only one good cause, Bill, for poor blokes
    like us to fight:
  That's self-defence, for 'earth and 'ome, and
    them that bears our name;
And that's wot I'm a-doin' by the sandbags 'ere
    to-night. . . .
  But Fritz out there will tell you 'e's a-doin' of
    the same.

Starin' over the sandbags,
  Sick of the 'ole dam thing;
Firin' to keep meself awake,
  'Earin' the bullets sing.

76

A SONG OF THE SANDBAGS

(Hiss! Twang! Tsing! Pang!
  Saucy the bullets sing.)
Dreamin' 'ere by the sandbags
  Of a day when war will cease,
When 'Ans and Fritz and Bill and me
Will clink our mugs in fraternity,
And the Brotherhood of Labour will be
  The Brotherhood of Peace.

ON THE WIRE

Oh God! take the sun from the sky!
  It's burning me, scorching me up.
God, can't You hear my cry?
  Water! A poor, little cup!
It's laughing, the cursèd sun!
  See how it swells and swells
  Fierce as a hundred hells!
God, will it never have done?
It's searing the flesh on my bones;
  It's beating with hammers red
  My eyeballs into my head;
It's parching my very moans.
See! it's the size of the sky,
  And the sky is a torrent of fire
Foaming on me as I lie
  Here on the wire . . . the wire. . . .

Of the thousands that wheeze and hum
  Heedlessly over my head,
Why can't a bullet come,
  Pierce to my brain instead;

ON THE WIRE

Blacken forever my brain,
Finish forever my pain?
  Here in the hellish glare
Why must I suffer so?
  Is it God doesn't care?
Is it God doesn't know?
    Oh! to be killed outright,
    Clean in the clash of the fight!
That is a golden death,
    That is a boon, but this. . . .
Drawing an anguished breath
    Under a hot abyss,
Under a stooping sky
    Of seething, sulphurous fire,
Scorching me up as I lie
    Here on the wire . . . the wire. . . .

Hasten, Oh God! Thy night!
Hide from my eyes the sight
Of the body I stare and see
Shattered so hideously.
I can't believe that it's mine.
    My body was white and sweet,
Flawless and fair and fine,
    Shapeless from head to feet;

ON THE WIRE

Oh, no, I can never be
The thing of horror I see
Under the rifle fire,
Trussed on the wire . . . the wire. . . .

Of night and of death I dream,
   Night that will bring me peace,
Coolness and starry gleam,
   Stillness and death's release;
Ages and ages have passed,—
Lo! it is night at last.
   Night! but the guns roar out;
Night! but the hosts attack.
Red and yellow and black,
   Geysers of doom upspout.
Silver and green and red,
Star-shells hover and spread.
Yonder off to the right
Fiercely kindles the fight;
Roaring near and more near,
Thundering now in my ear;
Close to me, close. . . . Oh, hark!
Someone moans in the dark.
I hear, but I cannot see;
   I hear as the rest retire,
Someone is caught like me,
   Caught on the wire . . . the wire. . . .

ON THE WIRE

Again the shuddering dawn,
Weird and wicked and wan;
Again, and I've not yet gone,
The man whom I heard is dead.
   Now I can understand:
A bullet hole in his head,
   A pistol gripped in his hand.
Well, he knew what to do—
Yes, and now I know, too. . . .

Hark, the resentful guns!
   Oh how thankful am I
To think my belovèd ones
   Will never know how I die!
I've suffered more than my share;
I'm shattered beyond repair;
I've fought like a man the fight,
And now I demand the right
(God! how his fingers cling!)
To do without shame this thing.
Good! there's a bullet still;
   Now I'm ready to fire;
Blame me, God, if You will,
   Here on the wire . . . the wire. . .

BILL'S GRAVE

I'M gatherin' flowers by the wayside to lay on the
grave of Bill;
I've sneaked away from the billet, 'cause Jim
wouldn't understand;
'E'd call me a silly fat'ead, and larf till it made
'im ill,
To see me 'ere in the cornfield, wiv a big bookay
in me 'and.

For Jim and me we are rough 'uns, but Bill was
one o' the best;
We 'listed and learned together to larf at the
wust wot comes;
Then Bill copped a packet proper, and took 'is
departure West,
So sudden 'e 'adn't a minit to say good-bye to
'is chums.

BILL'S GRAVE

And they took me to where 'e was planted, a sort
    of a measly mound;
  And thinks I, 'ow Bill would be tickled, bein'
    so soft and queer,
If I gathered a bunch o' them wild-flowers, and
    sort of arranged them round
  Like a kind of a bloody headpiece . . . .
    and that's the reason I'm here.

But not for the love of glory I wouldn't 'ave Jim
    to know.
  'E'd call me a slobberin' Cissy, and larf till 'is
    sides was sore;
I'd 'ave larfed at meself too, it isn't so long ago;
  But some'ow it changes a feller, 'avin' a taste
    o' war.

It 'elps a man to be 'elpful, to know wot 'is pals
    is worth;
  (Them golden poppies is blazin' like lamps
    some fairy 'as lit)
I'm fond o' them big white dysies. . . . Now,
    Jim's o' the salt o' the earth
  But 'e 'as got a tongue wot's a terror, and 'e
    ain't sentimental a bit.

BILL'S GRAVE

I likes them blue chaps wot's 'idin' so shylike
    among the corn,
    Won't Bill be glad! We was allus thicker 'n
    thieves, us three.
Why! 'oo's that singin' so 'earty? *Jim!* And as
    sure as I'm born
    'E's there in the giddy corn-fields, a-gatherin'
    flowers like me.

Quick! drop me posy be'ind me. I watches 'im
    for a while,
    Then I says: " Wot 'o, there, Chummy! Wot
    price the little bookay?"
And 'e starts like a bloke wot's guilty, and 'e says
    with a sheepish smile:
    " She's a bit of orl right, the widder wot keeps
    the estaminay."

So 'e goes away in a 'urry, and I wishes 'im best
    o' luck,
    And I picks up me bunch o' wild-flowers, and
    the light's gettin' sorto dim
When I makes me way to the boneyard, and
    . . . . I stares like a man wot's stuck,
    For wot do I see? *Bill's grave-mound strewn
    with the flowers of Jim.*

BILL'S GRAVE

Of course I won't never tell 'im, bein' a tactical
    lad;
  And Jim parley-voos to the widder: "Trez
    beans, lamoor; compree?"
Oh, 'e'd die of shame if 'e knew I knew; but say!
    won't Bill be glad
  When 'e stares through the bleedin' clods and
    sees the blossoms of Jim and me?

JEAN DESPREZ

Oh ye whose hearts are resonant, and ring to
War's romance,
Hear ye the story of a boy, a peasant boy of
France;
A lad uncouth and warped with toil, yet who,
when trial came,
Could feel within his soul upleap and soar the
sacred flame;
Could stand upright, and scorn and smite, as
only heroes may:
Oh, harken! Let me try to tell the tale of Jean
Desprez.

With fire and sword the Teuton horde was ravag-
ing the land,
And there was darkness and despair, grim death
on every hand;
Red fields of slaughter sloping down to ruin's
black abyss;
The wolves of war ran evil-fanged, and little did
they miss.

86

JEAN DESPREZ

And on they came with fear and flame, to burn
and loot and slay,
Until they reached the red-roofed croft, the home
of Jean Desprez.

" Rout out the village, one and all!" the Uhlan
Captain said.
" Behold!   Some hand has fired a shot.   My
trumpeter is dead.
Now shall they Prussian vengeance know; now
shall they rue the day,
For by this sacred German slain, ten of these
dogs shall pay."
They drove the cowering peasants forth, women
and babes and men,
And from the last, with many a jeer the Cap-
tain chose he ten;
Ten simple peasants, bowed with toil; they stood,
they knew not why
Against the grey wall of the church, hearing
their children cry;
Hearing their wives and mothers wail, with faces
dazed they stood.
A moment only . . . *Ready!* *Fire!* They
weltered in their blood.

JEAN DESPREZ

But there was one who gazed unseen, who heard
  the frenzied cries,
Who saw these men in sabots fall before their
  children's eyes;
A Zouave, wounded, in a ditch, and knowing
  death was nigh,
He laughed with joy: " Ah! here is where I settle
  ere I die."
He clutched his rifle once again, and long he
  aimed and well . . .
A shot! Beside his victims ten the Uhlan Captain fell.

They dragged the wounded Zouave out; their
  rage was like a flame.
With bayonets they pinned him down, until their
  Major came.
A blonde, full-blooded man he was, and arrogant
  of eye;
He stared to see with shattered skull his favour-
  ite Captain lie.
" Nay, do not finish him so quick, this foreign
  swine," he cried;
" Go nail him to the big church door: he shall be
  crucified."

JEAN DESPREZ

With bayonets through hands and feet they
    nailed the Zouave there,
And there was anguish in his eyes, and horror in
    his stare;
"Water! A single drop!" he moaned; but how
    they jeered at him,
And mocked him with an empty cup, and saw his
    sight grow dim;
And as in agony of death with blood his lips were
    wet,
The Prussian Major gaily laughed, and lit a
    cigarette.

But 'mid the white-faced villagers who cowered
    in horror by,
Was one who saw the woeful sight, who heard the
    woeful cry:
"Water! One little drop, I beg! For love of
    Christ who died. . ."
It was the little Jean Desprez who turned and
    stole aside;
It was the little bare-foot boy who came with cup
    abrim
And walked up to the dying man, and gave the
    drink to him.

JEAN DESPREZ

A roar of rage! They seize the boy; they tear
    him fast away.
The Prussian Major swings around; no longer is
    he gay.
His teeth are wolfishly agleam; his face all dark
    with spite:
" Go, shoot the brat," he snarls, " that dare defy
    our Prussian might.
Yet stay! I have another thought. I'll kindly be,
    and spare;
Quick! give the lad a rifle charged, and set him
    squarely there,
And bid him shoot, and shoot to kill. Haste!
    Make him understand
The dying dog he fain would save shall perish by
    his hand;
And all his kindred they shall see, and all shall
    curse his name,
Who bought his life at such a cost, the price of
    death and shame."

They brought the boy, wild-eyed with fear; they
    made him understand;
They stood him by the dying man, a rifle in his
    hand.

JEAN DESPREZ

"Make haste!" said they; "the time is short,
  and you must kill or die."
The Major puffed his cigarette, amusement in his
  eye.
And then the dying Zouave heard, and raised his
  weary head:
"Shoot, son, 'twill be the best for both; shoot
  swift and straight," he said;
"Fire first and last, and do not flinch, for lost to
  hope am I;
And I will murmur: 'Vive La France!' and bless
  you ere I die."

Half-blind with blows the boy stood there; he
  seemed to swoon and sway;
Then in that moment woke the soul of little Jean
  Desprez.
He saw the woods go sheening down; the larks
  were singing clear;
And oh the scents and sounds of Spring, how
  sweet they were! how dear!
He felt the scent of new-mown hay, a soft breeze
  fanned his brow;
Oh God! the paths of peace and toil! How pre-
  cious were they now!

JEAN DESPREZ

The Summer days and Summer ways, how bright
    they were with bliss!
The Autumn such a dream of gold. . . . and
    all must end in this:
This shining rifle in his hand, that shambles all
    around;
The Zouave there with dying glare; the blood
    upon the ground;
The brutal faces 'round him ringed, the evil eyes
    aflame;
That Prussian bully standing by, as if he watched
    a game.
" Make haste and shoot," the Major sneered; " a
    minute more I give;
A minute more to kill your friend, if you yourself
    would live."

They only saw a barefoot boy, with blanched and
    twitching face;
They did not see within his eyes the glory of his
    race;
The glory of a million men who for fair France
    have died,
The splendour of self-sacrifice that will not be
    denied.

JEAN DESPREZ

Yet . . . he was but a peasant lad, and oh!
    but life was sweet . . .
"Your minute's nearly gone, my lad," he heard
    a voice repeat.
"Shoot! shoot!" the dying Zouave moaned;
    "Shoot! shoot!" the soldiers said:
Then Jean Desprez reached out and shot . . .
    the Prussian Major dead.

GOING HOME

I'M goin' 'ome to Blighty—ain't I glad to 'ave the
    chance!
I'm loaded up wiv fightin', and I've 'ad my fill o'
    France;
I'm feelin' so excited like, I want to sing and
    dance,
    For I'm goin' 'ome to Blighty in the mawnin'.

I'm goin' 'ome to Blighty: can you wonder as I'm
    gay?
I've got a wound I wouldn't sell for 'alf a year o'
    pay;
A harm that's mashed to jelly in the nicest sort
    o' way,
    For it takes me 'ome to Blighty in the mawnin'.

'Ow everlastin' keen I was on gettin' to the front!
I'd ginger for a dozen, and I 'elped to bear the
    brunt;
But Cheese and Crust! I'm crazy, now I've done
    me little stunt,
    To sniff the air of Blighty in the mawnin'.

GOING HOME

I've looked upon the wine that's white, and on
    the wine that's red;
I've looked on cider flowin', till it fairly turned
    me 'ead;
But oh! the finest scoff will be, when all is done
    and said,
  A pint o' Bass in Blighty in the mawnin'!

I'm goin' back to Blighty, which I left to strafe
    the 'Un;
I've fought in bloody battles, and I've 'ad a 'eap
    of fun;
But now me flipper's busted, and I think me
    dooty's done,
  And I'll kiss me gel in Blighty in the mawnin'.

Oh, there be furrin lands to see, and some of 'em
    be fine;
And there be furrin gels to kiss, and scented
    furrin wine;
But there's no land like England, and no other
    gel like mine:
  Thank Gawd for dear old Blighty in the
  mawnin'.

COCOTTE

WHEN a girl's sixteen, and as poor as she's pretty,
And she hasn't a friend and she hasn't a home,
Heigh-ho! She's as safe in Paris city
As a lamb night-strayed where the wild wolves
roam;
And that was I. Oh! it's seven years now;
(Some water's run down the Seine since then),
And I've almost forgotten the pangs and the
tears now,
And I've almost taken the measure of men.

Oh! I found me a lover who loved me only,
Artist and poet and almost a boy.
And my heart was bruised, and my life was
lonely,
And him I adored with a wonderful joy.
If he'd come to me with his pockets empty,
How we'd have laughed in a garret gay!
But he was rich and in radiant plenty
We lived in a villa at Viroflay.

COCOTTE

Then came the War, and of bliss bereft me;
  Then came the call, and he went away;
All that he had in the world he left me,
  With the rose-wreathed villa at Viroflay.
Then came the news and the tragic story:
  My hero, my splendid lover, was dead,
Sword in hand on the field of glory,
  And he died with my name on his lips, they
    said.

So here am I in my widow's mourning,
  The weeds I've really no right to wear;
And women fix me with eyes of scorning,
  Call me " cocotte," but I do not care.
And men look at me with eyes that borrow
  The brightness of love, but I turn away;
Alone, say I, I will live with Sorrow,
  In my little villa at Viroflay.

And lo! I'm living alone with—*Pity*,
  And they say that pity from love's not far;
Let me tell you all: Last week in the city
  I took the Metro. at Saint Lazare;
And the carriage was crowded to overflowing,
  And when there entered at Chateaudun
Two wounded *poilus* with medals showing,
  I eagerly gave my seat to one.

7   97

COCOTTE

You should have seen them: they'd slipped death's
    clutches,
  But sadder a sight you will rarely find;
One had a leg off and walked on crutches,
  The other, a bit of a boy, was blind.
And they both sat down, and the lad was trying
  To grope his way as a blind man tries;
And half of the women around were crying,
  And some of the men had tears in their eyes.

How he stirred me, this blind boy, clinging
  Just like a child to his crippled chum.
But I did not cry. Oh, no! a singing
  Came to my heart for a year so dumb.
Then I knew that at three-and-twenty
  There is wonderful work to be done,
Comfort and kindness and joy in plenty,
  Peace and light and love to be won.

Oh, thought I, could mine eyes be given
  To one who will live in the dark alway!
To love and to serve—'twould make life Heaven
  Here in my villa at Viroflay.
So I left my *poilus:* and now you wonder
  Why to-day I am so elate. . . .
Look! In the glory of sunshine yonder
  They're bringing my blind boy in at the gate.

MY BAY'NIT

WHEN first I left Blighty they gave me a bay'nit
  And told me it 'ad to be smothered wiv gore;
But Blimey! I 'aven't been able to stain it,
  So far as I've gone, wiv the vintage of war.
For ain't it a fraud! when a Boche and yours
    truly
  Gits into a mix in the grit and the grime,
He jerks up 'is 'ands wiv a yell and 'e's duly
  Part of me outfit every time.

      Left, right, Hans and Fritz!
      Goose step, keep up yer mits!
      Oh my! ain't it a shyme?
      Part of me outfit every time.

MY BAY'NIT

At toasting a biscuit me bay'nit's a dandy;
   I've used it to open a bully beef can;
For pokin' the fire it comes in werry 'andy;
   For any old thing but for stickin' a man.
'Ow often I've said: " 'Ere, I'm goin' to press you
   Into a 'Un till you're seasoned for prime;
And fiercely I rushes to do it, but bless you!
   Part of me outfit every time.

     Lor', yus, *don't* they look glad!
     Right O! 'Owl Kamerad!
     Oh my! always the syme,
     Part of me outfit every time.

I'm 'untin' for someone to christen me bay'nit,
   Some nice juicy Chewton wot's fightin' in
      France;
I'm fairly down'earted; 'ow *can* yer explain it?
   I keeps gettin' prisoners every chance.
As soon as they sees me they ups and surrenders,
   Extended like monkeys wot's tryin' to climb;
And I uses me bay'nit—to slit their suspenders:
   Part of me outfit every time.

     Four 'Uns; lor', wot a bag!
     'Ere, Fritz, sample a fag!
     Oh my! ain't it a gyme!
     Part of me outfit every time.

CARRY ON

It's easy to fight when everything's right,
  And you're mad with the thrill and the glory;
It's easy to cheer when victory's near,
  And wallow in fields that are gory.
It's a different song when everything's wrong,
  When you're feeling infernally mortal;
When it's ten against one, and hope there is none,
  Buck up, little soldier, and chortle:

    Carry on! Carry on!
    There isn't much punch in your blow.
You're glaring and staring and hitting out blind;
You're muddy and bloody, but never you mind;
    Carry on! Carry on!
    You haven't the ghost of a show;
It's looking like death, but while you've a breath,
    Carry on, my son! Carry on!

CARRY ON

And so in the strife of the battle of life,
   It's easy to fight when you're winning;
It's easy to slave and starve and be brave
   When the dawn of success is beginning;
But the man who can meet despair and defeat
   With a cheer—there's the man of God's choos-
      ing;
The man who can fight to Heaven's own height
   Is the man who can fight when he's losing.

     Carry on! Carry on!
   Things never were looming so black.
But show that you haven't a cowardly streak,
And though you're unlucky you never are weak;
     Carry on! Carry on!
   Brace up for another attack.
It's looking like hell, but—you never can tell—
   Carry on, old man! Carry on!

There are some who drift out in the deserts of
     doubt,
   And some who in brutishness wallow;
There are others I know who in piety go
   Because of a Heaven to follow.

CARRY ON

But to labour with zest and to give of your best,
  For the sweetness and joy of the giving,
To help folks along with a hand and a song:
  Why, there's the real sunshine of living.

    Carry on! Carry on!
   Fight the good fight and true.
Believe in your mission, greet life with a cheer;
There's big work to do, and that's why you are
  here.
    Carry on! Carry on!
   Let the world be the better for you;
And at last when you die, let this be your cry:
  Carry on, my soul! Carry on!

OVER THE PARAPET

ALL day long when the shells sail over
    I stand at the sandbags and take my chance;
But at night, at night I'm a reckless rover,
    And over the parapet gleams Romance.
Romance! Romance! How I've dreamed it, writ-
        ing
    Dreary old records of money and mart,
Me with my head chuckful of fighting
    And the blood of vikings to thrill my heart.

But little I thought that my time was coming,
    Sudden and splendid, supreme and soon.
And here I am with the bullets humming
    As I crawl and I curse the light of the moon.
Out alone, for adventure thirsting,
    Out in mysterious No Man's Land;
Prone with the dead when a star-shell bursting,
    Flares on the horrors on every hand.

OVER THE PARAPET

There are ruby stars and they drip and wiggle,
  And the grasses gleam in a light blood-red;
There are emerald stars, and their tails they
      wriggle,
  And ghastly they glare on the face of the dead.
But the worst of all are the stars of whiteness,
  That spill in a pool of pearly flame,
Pretty as gems in their silver brightness,
  And etching a man for a bullet's aim.

Yet oh! it's great to be here with danger,
  Here in the weird, death-pregnant dark,
In the devil's pasture a stealthy ranger,
  When the moon is decently hiding. Hark!
What was that? Was it just the shiver
  Of an eerie wind or a clammy hand?
The rustle of grass, or the passing quiver
  Of one of the ghosts of No Man's Land?

It's only at night when the ghosts awaken,
  And gibber and whisper horrible things;
For to every foot of this God-forsaken
  Zone of jeopard some horror clings.
Ugh! What was that? It felt like a jelly,
  That flattish mound in the noisome grass;
You three big rats running free of its belly,
  Out of my way and let me pass!

OVER THE PARAPET

But if there's horror, there's beauty, wonder;
    The trench lights gleam and the rockets play.
That flood of magnificent orange yonder
    Is a battery blazing miles away.
With a rush and a singing a great shell passes;
    The rifles resentfully bicker and brawl,
And here I crouch in the dew-drenched grasses,
    And look and listen and love it all.

God! What a life! But I must make haste now,
    Before the shadow of night be spent.
It's little the time there is to waste now,
    If I'd do the job for which I was sent.
My bombs are right and my clippers ready,
    And I wriggle out to the chosen place,
When I hear a rustle. . . . Steady! . . . .
        Steady!
    Who am I staring slap in the face?

There in the dark I can hear him breathing,
    A foot away, and as still as death;
And my heart beats hard, and my brain is seeth-
        ing,
    And I know he's a Hun by the smell of his
        breath.

OVER THE PARAPET

Then " Will you surrender?" I whisper hoarsely,
  For it's death, swift death to utter a cry.
" *English Schwein-hund!*" he murmurs coarsely.
  " Then we'll fight it out in the dark," say I.

So we grip and we slip and we trip and wrestle
  There in the gutter of No Man's Land;
And I feel my nails in his wind-pipe nestle,
  And he tries to gouge, but I bite his hand.
And he tries to squeal, but I squeeze him tighter:
  " Now," I say, " I can kill you fine;
But tell me first, you Teutonic blighter!
  Have you any children?" He answers: " Nein."

Nine! Well, I cannot kill such a father,
  So I tie his hands and I leave him there.
Do I finish my little job? Well, rather;
  And I get home safe with some light to spare.
Heigh-ho! by day it's just prosy duty,
  Doing the same old song and dance;
But oh! with the night—joy, glory, beauty;
  Over the parapet—Life, Romance.

THE BALLAD OF SOULFUL SAM

You want me to tell you a story, a yarn of the
firin' line,
Of our thin, red-kharki 'eroes, out there where
the bullets whine;
Out there where the bombs are bustin', and the
cannons like 'ell-doors slam—
Just order another drink, boys, and I'll tell you
of Soulful Sam.

Oh, Sam, he was never 'ilarious, though I've 'ad
some mates as was wus;
He 'adn't C.B. on his programme, he never was
known to cuss.
For a card or a skirt or a beer-mug he 'adn't a
friendly word,
But when it came down to Scriptures, say! wasn't
he just a bird!

THE BALLAD OF SOULFUL SAM

He always 'ad tracts in his pocket, the which he
 would haste to present,
And though the fellers would use them in ways
 that they never was meant,
I used to read 'em religious, and frequent I've
 been impressed
By some of them bundles of 'oly dope he carried
 around in his vest.

For I—and oh! 'ow I shudder at the 'orror the
 word conveys!—
'Ave been—let me whisper it 'oarsely—a gambler
 'alf of me days;
A gambler, you 'ear—a gambler. It makes me
 wishful to weep,
And yet 'ow it's true, my brethren—I'd rather
 gamble than sleep.

I've gambled the 'ole world over, from Monte
 Carlo to Maine;
From Dawson City to Dover, from San Francisco
 to Spain.
Cards! They 'ave been me ruin, they've taken
 me pride and me pelf,
And when I'd no one to play with, why, I'd go
 and I'd play by meself.

THE BALLAD OF SOULFUL SAM

And Sam 'e would sit and watch me, as I shuffled
    a greasy deck,
And 'e'd say: "You're bound to Perdition," and
    I'd answer: "Git off me neck."
And that's 'ow we came to get friendly, though
    built on a different plan,
Me wot's a desprite gambler, 'im sich a good
    young man.

But on to me tale. Just imagine. . . . Dark-
    ness! The battle-front!
The furious 'Uns attackin'! Us ones a-bearin'
    the brunt!
Me crouchin' be'ind a sandbag, tryin' 'ard to keep
    calm,
When I 'ears someone singin' a 'ymn toon;—
    behold! it is Soulful Sam.

Yes, right in the crash of the combat, in the fury
    of flash and flame,
'E was shootin' and singin' serenely as if 'e
    enjoyed the same;
And there in the 'eat of the battle, as the 'ordes
    of demons attacked,
He dipped down into 'is tunic, and 'e 'anded me
    out a tract.

THE BALLAD OF SOULFUL SAM

Then a star-shell flared, and I read it: "Oh! flee
from the wrath to come!"
Nice cheerful subject, I tell yer, when you're
'earin' the bullets 'um.
Then before I 'ad time to thank 'im, just one of
them bits of lead
Comes slingin' along in a 'urry, and it 'its my
partner. . . . Dead?

No, siree! Not by a long sight! For it plugged
'im 'ard on the chest,
Just where 'e'd tracts for a harmy corps stowed
away in 'is vest.
On its mission of death that bullet 'ustled along
and it caved
A 'ole in them tracts to 'is 'ide, boys—but the life
o' me pal was saved.

And there as 'e showed me in triumph, and 'orror
was chokin' me breath,
On came another bullet on its 'orrible mission of
death;
On through the night it cavorted, seekin' its 'aven
of rest,
And it zipped through a crack in the sandbags,
and it wolloped me bang on the breast.

THE BALLAD OF SOULFUL SAM

Was I killed, do you ask? Oh no, boys. Why am
     I sittin' 'ere,
Gazin' with mournful vision at a mug long empty
     of beer?
With a throat as dry as a—— Oh, thanky! I
     don't much mind if I do.
Beer with a dash of 'Ollands, that's my particu-
     lar brew.

Oh, that was a terrible moment. It 'ammered me
     'ard o'er the 'eart.
It bowled me down like a nine-pin, and I looked
     for the blood to start.
And I saw in the flash of a moment, in that thun-
     der of hate and strife,
Me wretched past like a pitchur, the sins of a
     gambler's life.

For I 'ad no tracts to save me, to thwart that mad
     missile's doom;
I 'ad no pious pamphlets to 'elp me to cheat the
     tomb;
I 'ad no 'oly leaflets to baffle a bullet's aim;
I'd only—a deck of cards, boys, but . . . . .
     it seemed to do just the same.

ONLY A BOCHE

WE brought him in from between the lines; we'd
    better have let him lie;
For what's the use of risking one's skin for a *type*
    that's going to die?
What s the use of tearing him loose under a
    gruelling fire,
When he's shot in the head, and worse than dead,
    and all messed up on the wire?
However, I say, we brought him in. *Diable!* The
    mud was bad;
The trench was crooked and greasy and high, and
    oh! what a time we had!
And often we slipped, and often we tripped, but
    never he made a moan;
And how we were wet with blood and with sweat,
    but we carried him in like our own.

Now there he lies in the dug-out dim, awaiting
    the ambulance,
And the doctor shrugs his shoulders at him, and
    remarks, " He hasn't a chance."

8

ONLY A BOCHE

And we squat and smoke at our game of bridge
  on the glistening, straw-packed floor.
And above our oaths we can hear his breath deep-
  drawn in a kind of snore.
For the dressing station is long and low, and the
  candles gutter dim,
And the mean light falls on the cold clay walls
  and our faces bristly and grim;
And we flap our cards on the lousy straw, and we
  laugh and jibe as we play,
And you'd never know that the cursèd foe was
  less than a mile away.
As we con our cards in the rancid gloom,
  oppressed by that snoring breath,
You'd never dream that our broad roof-beam was
  swept by the broom of death.

Heigh-ho! My turn for the dummy hand; I rise
  and I stretch a bit;
The fetid air is making me yawn, and my cigarette's unlit,
So I go to the nearest candle flame, and the man
  we brought is there,
And his face is white in the shabby light, and I
  stand at his feet and stare.

ONLY A BOCHE

Stand for awhile, and quietly stare, for strange
    though it seems to be,
The dying Boche on the stretcher there has a
    queer resemblance to me.

It gives one a kind of turn, you know, to come
    on a thing like that,
It's just as if I were lying there, with a turban
    of blood for a hat;
Lying there in a coat grey-green instead of a coat
    grey-blue,
With one of my eyes all shot away, and my brain
    half tumbling through;
Lying there with a chest that heaves like a bel-
    lows up and down,
And a cheek as white as snow on a grave, and lips
    that are coffee-brown.

And confound him, too! He wears like me on his
    finger a wedding ring,
And around his neck, as around my own, by a
    greasy bit of string,
A locket hangs with a woman's face, and I turn
    it about to see:
Just as I thought . . . . on the other side
    the faces of children three;

ONLY A BOCHE

Clustered together cherub-like, three little laugh-
    ing girls,
With the usual tiny rosebud mouths and the
    usual silken curls.
"Zut!" I say, "he has beaten me; for me, I have
    only two,"
And I push the locket beneath his shirt, feeling
    a little blue.

Oh! it isn't cheerful to see a man, the marvellous
    work of God,
Crushed in the mutilation mill, crushed to a
    smeary clod;
Oh! it isn't cheerful to hear him moan; but it
    isn't that I mind;
It isn't the anguish that goes with him, it's the
    anguish he leaves behind;
For his going opens a tragic door that gives one
    a world of pain,
And the death he dies, those who live and love,
    will die again and again.

So here I am at my cards once more, but it's kind
    of spoiling my play,
Thinking of those three brats of his so many a
    mile away.

ONLY A BOCHE

War is war, and he's only a Boche, and we all of
 us take our chance;
But all the same I'll be mighty glad when I'm
 hearing the ambulance.
One foe the less, but all the same I'm heartily
 glad I'm not
The man who gave him his broken head, the
 sniper who fired the shot.

No trumps you make it, I think you said? You'll
 pardon me if I err;
For a moment I thought of other things—*Mon
 Dieu! Quelle vache de guerre.*

PILGRIMS

For oh! when the war will be over,
  We'll go and we'll look for our dead;
We'll go when the bee's on the clover,
  And the plume of the poppy is red;
We'll go when the year's at its gayest,
  When meadows are laughing with flow'rs;
And there where the crosses are grayest,
  We'll seek for the cross that is ours.

For they cry to us: *Friends, we are lonely,*
  A-weary the night and the day;
But come in the blossom-time only,
  Come when our graves will be gay:
When daffodils all are a-blowing,
  And larks are a-thrilling the skies,
Oh, come with the hearts of you glowing,
  And the joy of the Spring in your eyes.

PILGRIMS

But never, oh! never come sighing,
  For ours was the Splendid Release;
And oh! but 'twas joy in the dying
  To know we were winning you Peace.
So come when the valleys are sheening,
  And fledged with the promise of grain;
And here where our graves will be greening,
  Just smile and be happy again.

And so when the war will be over,
  We'll seek for the Wonderful One;
And maiden will look for her lover,
  And mother will look for her son;
And there will be end to our grieving,
  And gladness will gleam over loss,
As—glory beyond all believing!—
  We point . . . . to a name on a cross.

119

MY PRISONER

WE was in a crump-'ole, 'im and me;
Fightin' wiv our bayonets was we;
Fightin' 'ard as 'ell we was,
Fightin' fierce as fire because
    It was 'im or me as must be downed;
'E was twice as big as me;
I was 'arf the weight of 'e;
    We was like a terryer and a 'ound.

'Struth! But 'e was sich a 'andsome bloke.
Me, I'm 'andsome as a chunk o' coke.
Did I give it 'im? Not 'arf!
Why, it fairly made me laugh,
    'Cos 'is bloomin' bellows wasn't sound.
Couldn't fight for monkey-nuts,
Soon I gets 'im in the guts,
    There 'e lies a-floppin' on the ground.

MY PRISONER

In I goes to finish up the job.
Quick 'e throws 'is 'ands above 'is nob;
Speakin' English good as me:
" 'Tain't no use to kill," says 'e;
  " Can't yer tyke me prisoner instead?"
" Why, I'd like to, sir," says I;
" But—yer knows the reason why:
  If we pokes our noses out we're dead.

" Sorry, sir. Then on the other 'and
(As a gent like you must understand),
If I 'olds you longer 'ere,
Wiv yer pals so werry near,
  It's me 'oo'll 'ave a free trip to Berlin;
If I lets yer go away,
Why, you'll fight another day:
  See the sitooation I am in.

" Anyway, I'll tell you wot I'll do,
Bein' kind and seein' as it's you,
Knowin' 'ow it's cold, the feel
Of a 'alf a yard o' steel,
  I'll let yer 'ave a rifle ball instead;
Now, jist think yerself in luck. . . .
'Ere, ol' man! You keep 'em stuck,
  Them saucy dooks o' yours, above yer 'ead."

MY PRISONER

'Ow 'is mits shot up it made me smile.
'Ow 'e seemed to ponder for a while.
Then 'e says: " It seems a shyme,
Me, a man wot's known ter fyme:
Give me blocks of stone, I'll give yer—gods.
Whereas, pardon me, I'm sure
You, my friend, are still obscure. . . ."
"In war," says I, "that makes no blurry
odds."

Then says 'e: " I've painted picters too. . . .
Oh, dear God! The work I planned to do,
And to think this is the end!"
"'Ere," says I, "my hartist friend,
Don't you give yerself no friskin' airs.
Picters, statoos, is that why
You should be let off to die?
That the best ye done? Just say yer prayers."

Once again 'e seems ter think awhile.
Then 'e smiles a werry 'aughty smile:
"Why, no, sir, it's not the best;
There's a locket next me breast,
Picter of a gel 'oo's eyes are blue.
That's the best I've done," says 'e;
" That's me darter, aged three. . . ."
"Blimey!" says I, " I've a nipper too."

MY PRISONER

Straight I chucks my rifle to one side;
Shows 'im wiv a lovin' father's pride,
Me own little Mary Jane,
Proud 'e shows me 'is Elaine,
    And we talks as friendly as can be;
Then I 'elps 'im on 'is way,
'Opes 'e's sife at 'ome to-day,
    Wonders—*'ow would 'e 'ave treated me?*

TRI-COLOUR

Poppies, you try to tell me, glowing there in the
     wheat;
  Poppies! Ah no! You mock me: it's blood, I
     tell you, it's blood.
It's gleaming wet in the grasses, it's glist'ning
     warm in the wheat,
  It dabbles the ferns and the clover, it brims in
     an angry flood;
It leaps to the startled heavens, it smothers the
     sun, it cries
  With scarlet voices of triumph from blossom
     and bough and blade.
See the bright horror of it! It's roaring out of
     the skies,
  And the whole red world is a-welter. . . .
     Oh God! I'm afraid, I'm afraid.

Cornflowers, you say, just cornflowers, gemming
     the golden grain;
  Ah, no! You can't deceive me. Can't I believe
     my eyes?

TRI-COLOUR

Look! It's the dead, my comrades, stark on the
    dreadful plain,
    All in their dark-blue blouses, staring up at the
      skies.
Comrades of canteen laughter, dumb in the yel-
    low wheat,
    See how they sprawl and huddle! See how
      their brows are white!
Goaded on to the shambles, there in death and
    defeat. . . .
    Father of Pity, hide them! Hasten, O God,
      Thy night!

Lilies (the light is waning), only lilies, you say,
    Nestling and softly shining there where the
      spear-grass waves.
No, my friend, I know better; brighter I see than
    day:
    It's the poor little wooden crosses over their
      quiet graves.
Oh, how they're gleaming, gleaming! See! Each
    cross has a crown.
    Yes, it's true, I am dying,—little will be the
      loss. . . .
Darkness. . . . but look! In Heaven, a light,
    and it's shining down. . . .
    God's accolade! Lift me up, friends. I'm
      going to win—*my Cross.*

A POT OF TEA

You make it in your mess-tin by the brazier's
    rosy gleam;
  You watch it cloud, then settle amber clear;
You lift it with your bay'nit, and you sniff the
    fragrant steam,
  The very breath of it is ripe with cheer.
You're awful cold and dirty, and a-cursing of
    your lot;
You scoff the blushin' 'alf of it, so rich and rip-
    ping hot;
It bucks you up like anythink, just seems to touch
    the spot:
  God bless the man that first discovered Tea.

Since I came out to fight in France (which ain't
    the other day),
  I think I've drunk enough to float a barge;
All kinds of fancy foreign dope, from caffy and
    doo lay,
  To rum they serves you out before a charge;

A POT OF TEA

In back rooms of estaminays I've gurgled pints
     of cham;
I've swilled down mugs of cider till I've felt a
     bloomin' dam;
But s'truth! they all ain't in it with the vintage
     of Assam;
     God bless the man that first invented Tea.

I think them lazy lumps o' gods wot kips on
     asphodel
     Swigs nectar that's a flavour of Oolong;
I only wish them sons o' guns a-grillin' down in
     'ell
     Could have their daily ration of Suchong.
Hurrah! I'm off to battle, which is 'ell and 'eaven
     too;
And if I don't give some poor bloke a sexton's
     job to do,
To-night by Fritz's campfire won't I 'ave a gorge-
     ous brew,
     (For fightin' mustn't interfere with Tea).
To-night we'll all be telling of the Boches that we
     slew,
     As we drink the giddy victory in Tea.

THE REVELATION

*The same old sprint in the morning, boys, to the
same old din and smut;*
*Chained all day to the same old desk, down in the
same old rut;*
*Posting the same old greasy books, catching the
same old train:*
*Oh, how will I manage to stick it all, if I ever get
back again?*

We've bidden good-bye to life in a cage, we're finished with pushing a pen;
They're pumping us full of bellicose rage, they're
showing us how to be men;
We're only beginning to find ourselves; we're
wonders of brawn and thew;
But when we go back to our Cissy jobs, Oh!
what are we going to do?

THE REVELATION

For shoulders curved with the counter stoop will
    be carried erect and square,
And faces white from the office light will be
    bronzed by the open air;
And we'll walk with the stride of a new-born
    pride, with a new-found joy in our eyes,
Scornful men who have diced with death under
    the naked skies.

And when we get back to the dreary grind, and
    the bald-headed boss's call,
Don't you think that the dingy window-blind, and
    the dingier office wall
Will suddenly melt to a vision of space, of violent,
    flame-scarred night?
Then . . . Oh! the joy of the danger-thrill,
    and oh! the roar of the fight!

Don't you think as we peddle a card of pins the
    counter will fade away,
And again we'll be seeing the sand-bag rims, and
    the barb-wire's misty grey?
As a flat voice asks for a pound of tea don't you
    fancy we'll hear instead
The night-wind moan and the soothing drone of
    the packet that's overhead.

9

THE REVELATION

Don't you guess that the things we're seeing now
    will haunt us through all the years;
Heaven and hell rolled into one, glory and blood
    and tears;
Life's pattern picked with a scarlet thread, where
    once we wove with a grey,
To remind us all how we played our part in the
    shock of an epic day.

Oh, we're booked for the Great Adventure now,
    we're pledged to the Real Romance;
We'll find ourselves or we'll lose ourselves some-
    where in giddy old France.
We'll know the zest of the fighter's life; the best
    that we have we'll give,
We'll hunger and thirst; we'll die, . . . but
    first—we'll live, by the gods, we'll live!

We'll breathe free air and we'll bivouac under
    the starry sky;
We'll march with men, and we'll fight with men,
    and we'll see men laugh and die;
We'll know such joy as we never dreamed; we'll
    fathom the deeps of pain;
But the hardest bit of it all will be—when we
    come back home again.

THE REVELATION

For some of us smirk in a chiffon shop, and some
  of us teach in a school;
Some of us help with the seat of our pants to
  polish an office stool;
The merits of somebody's soap or jam some of us
  seek to explain,
But all of us wonder what we'll do when we have
  to go back again.

GRAND-PÈRE

AND so when he reached my bed
  The General made a stand:
"My brave young fellow," he said,
  "I would shake your hand."

So I lifted my arm, the right,
  With never a hand at all;
Only a stump, a sight
  Fit to appal.

"Well, well. Now that's too bad!
  That's sorrowful luck," he said;
"But there! You give me, my lad,
  The left instead."

So from under the blanket's rim
  I raised and showed him the other,
A snag as ugly and grim
  As its ugly brother.

132

GRAND-PÈRE

He looked at each jagged wrist,
    He looked, but he did not speak;
And then he bent down and kissed
    Me on either cheek.

You wonder now I don't mind
    I hadn't a hand to offer;
They tell me (you know I'm blind)
    'Twas Grand-père Joffre.

SON

He hurried away, young heart of joy, under our
    Devon sky!
And I watched him go, my beautiful boy, and a
    wary woman was I.
For my hair is grey, and his was gold; he'd the
    best of his life to live,
And I'd loved him so, and I'm old, I'm old, and
    he's all I had to give.

Ah yes, he was proud and swift and gay; but oh!
    how my eyes were dim!
With the sun in his heart he went away, but he
    took the sun with him.
For look!   How the leaves are falling now, and
    the Winter won't be long . . .
Oh! boy, my boy with the sunny brow, and the
    lips of love and of song!

134

SON

How we used to sit at the day's sweet end, we two
    by the firelight's gleam;
And we'd drift to the Valley of Let's Pretend, on
    the Bountiful River of Dream.
Oh, dear little heart! All wealth untold would I
    gladly, gladly pay
Could I just for a moment closely hold that
    golden head to my grey.

For I gaze in the fire, and I'm seeing there a
    child, and he waves to me;
And I run and I hold him up in the air, and he
    laughs and shouts with glee;
A little bundle of love and mirth, crying: " Come,
    Mumsie dear!"
Ah me! If he called from the ends of the earth
    I know that my heart would hear.

Yet the thought comes thrilling through all my
    pain: how worthier could he die?
Yea, a loss like that is a glorious gain, and pitiful
    proud am I.
For Peace must be bought with blood and tears,
    and the boys of our hearts must pay;
And so in our joy of the after years, let us bless
    them every day.

SON

And though I know there's a hasty grave with a
poor little cross at its head,
And the gold of his youth he so gladly gave, yet
to me he'll never be dead.
And the sun in my Devon lane will be gay, and
my boy will be with me still,
So I'm finding the heart to smile and say: "Oh
God, if it be Thy will!"

THE BLACK DUDEEN

Humping it here in the dug-out,
  Sucking me black dudeen,
I'd like to say, in a general way,
  There's nothing like Nickyteen;
There's nothing like Nickyteen, my boys,
  Be it pipes or snipes or cigars;
So be sure that a bloke
Has plenty to smoke,
  If you wants him to fight your wars.

When I've eat my fill and my belt is snug,
I begin to think of my baccy plug;
I whittle a fill in my horny palm,
And the bowl of me old clay pipe I cram.
I trim the edges, I tamp it down,
I nurse a light with an anxious frown;
I begin to draw, and my cheeks tuck in,
And all my face is a blissful grin:
And up in a cloud the good smoke goes,
And the good pipe glimmers and fades and glows;

THE BLACK DUDEEN

In its throat it chuckles a cheery song,
For I likes it hot and I likes it strong.
Oh! it's good is grub when you're feeling hollow,
But the best of a meal's the smoke to follow.

There was Micky and me on a night patrol,
Having to hide in a fizz-bang hole;
And sure I thought I was worse than dead,
Wi' them crump-crumps hustlin' over me head.
Sure I thought 'twas the dirty spot,
Hammer and tongs till the air was hot.
And, mind you, water up to your knees.
And cold! A monkey of brass would freeze.
And if we ventured our noses out
A " type-writer " clattered its pills about.
The Field of Glory! Well, I don't think!
I'd sooner be safe and snug in clink.

Then Micky, he goes and he cops one bad,
(He always was having ill luck, poor lad).
Says he: " Old chummy, I'm booked right
        through;
Death and me 'as a wrongday-voo.
But . . . 'aven't you got a pinch of shag?
I'd sell me perishin' soul for a fag."
And there he shivered and cussed his luck,
So I gave him me old black pipe to suck.

THE BLACK DUDEEN

And he heaves a sigh, and he takes to it
Like a babby takes to his mammy's tit;
Like an infant takes to his mother's breast,
Poor little Micky! he went to rest.

But the dawn was near, though the night was
    black,
So I left him there and I started back.
And I laughed as the silly old bullets came,
For the bullet ain't made wot's got me name.
Yet some of 'em buzzed onhealthily near,
And one little blighter just chipped me ear.
But there! I got to the trench all right,
When sudden I jumped wi' a start o' fright,
And a word that doesn't look well in type:
I'd clean forgotten me old clay pipe.

So I had to do it all over again,
Crawling out on that filthy plain.
Through shells and bombs and bullets and all—
Only this time I do not crawl.
I run like a man wot's missing a train,
Or a tom-cat caught in a plump of rain.
I hear the spit of a quick-fire gun
Tickle my heels, but I run, I run,
Through crash and crackle, and flicker and flame,
(Oh! the packet ain't issued wot's got me name!)

THE BLACK DUDEEN

I run like a man that's no ideer
Of hunting around for a sooveneer.
I run bang into a German chap,
And he stares like an owl, so I bash his map.
And just to show him that I'm his boss,
I gives him a kick on the parados;
And I marches him back with me all serene,
Wiv, tucked in me gub, me old dudeen.

Sitting here in the trenches
    Me heart's a-splittin' with spleen,
For a parcel o' lead comes missing me head,
    But it smashes me old dudeen.
God blast that red-headed sniper!
    I'll give him something to snipe;
Before the war's through
Just see how I do
    That blighter that smashed me pipe.

140

THE LITTLE PIOU-PIOU

Oh! some of us lolled in the château,
  And some of us slinked in the slum;
But now we are here with a song and a cheer
  To serve at the sign of the drum.
They put us in trousers of scarlet,
  ᵀn big sloppy ulsters of blue;
In boots that are flat, a box of a hat,
  And they call us the little piou-piou,
        Piou-piou,
The laughing and quaffing piou-piou,
The swinging and singing piou-piou;
And so with a rattle we march to the battle,
The weary but cheery piou-piou.

  Encore un petit verre de vin.
  Pour nous mettre en route;
  Encore un petit verre de vin
  Pour nous mettre en train.

THE LITTLE PIOU-PIOU

They drive us head-on for the slaughter;
    We haven't got much of a chance;
The issue looks bad, but we're awfully glad
    To battle and die for La France.
For some must be killed, that is certain;
    There's only one's duty to do;
So we leap to the fray in the glorious way
    They expect of the little piou-piou.
        En avant!
The way of the gallant piou-piou,
The dashing and smashing piou-piou;
The way grim and gory that leads us to glory
Is the way of the little piou-piou.

    Allons enfants de la Patrie,
    Le jour de gloire est arrivé.

To-day you would scarce recognize us,
    Such veterans war-wise are we;
So grimy and hard, so calloused and scarred,
    So " crummy," yet gay as can be.
We've finished with trousers of scarlet,
    They're giving us breeches of blue,
With a helmet instead of a cap on our head,—
    Yet still we're the little piou-piou.
        Nous les aurons!

THE LITTLE PIOU-PIOU

The jesting, unresting piou-piou,
The cheering, unfearing piou-piou;
The keep-your-head-level and fight-like-the-devil,
The dying, defying piou-piou.

> À la bayonette! Jusqu'a la mort!
> Sonnez la charge, clairons!

BILL THE BOMBER

THE poppies gleamed like bloody pools through
    cotton-woolly mist;
The Captain kept a-lookin' at the watch upon his
    wrist;
And there we smoked and squatted, as we watched
    the shrapnel flame;
'Twas wonnerful, I'm tellin' you, how fast them
    bullets came.
'Twas weary work the waiting, though; I tried to
    sleep a wink,
For waitin' means a-thinkin', and it doesn't do to
    think.
So I closed my eyes a little, and I had a niceish
    dream
Of a-standin' by a dresser with a dish of Devon
    cream;
But I hadn't time to sample it, for sudden-like I
    woke;
"Come on, me lads!" the Captain says, 'n I
    climbed out through the smoke.

BILL THE BOMBER

We spread out in the open: it was like a bath of
    lead;
But the boys they cheered and hollered fit to raise
    the bloody dead,
Till a beastly bullet copped 'em, then they lay
    without a sound,
And it's odd,—we didn't seem to 'eed them
    corpses on the ground.
And I kept on thinkin', thinkin', as the bullets
    faster flew,
How they picks the werry best men, and they lets
    the rotters through;
So indiscriminatin' like, they spares a man of sin,
And a rare lad wots a husband and a father gets
    done in.
And while havin' these reflections and advancin'
    on the run,
A bullet biffs me shoulder, and says I: " That's
    number one."

Well, it downed me for a jiffy, but I didn't lose
    me calm,
For I knew that I was needed; I'm a bomber, so
    I am.
I 'ad lost me cap and rifle, but I "carried on "
    because
I 'ad me bombs and knew that they was needed,
    so they was.

10

BILL THE BOMBER

We didn't 'ave no singin' now, nor many men to
  cheer;
Maybe the shrapnel drowned 'em, crashin' out so
  werry near;
And the Maxims got us sideways, and the bullets
  faster flew,
And I copped one on me flipper, and says I:
  "That's number two."

I was pleased it was the left one, for I 'ad me
  bombs, ye see,
And 'twas 'ard if they'd be wasted like, and all
  along o' me.
And I'd lost me 'at and rifle—but I told you that
  before,
So I packed me mit inside me coat and "carried
  on" once more.
But the rumpus it was wicked, and the men were
  scarcer yet,
And I felt me ginger goin', but me jaws I kinda
  set;
And we passed the Boche first trenches, which
  was 'eapin' 'igh with dead,
And we started for their second, which was fifty
  feet ahead,

146

BILL THE BOMBER

When somethink like a 'ammer smashed me
    savage on the knee,
And down I came all muck and blood. Says I:
    "That's number three."

So there I lay all 'elpless like, and bloody sick at
    that,
And worryin' like anythink, because I'd lost me
    'at;
And thinkin' of me missis, and the partin' words
    she said:
"If you gets killed, write quick, ol' man, and tell
    me as you're dead."
And lookin' at me bunch o' bombs,—that was the
    'ardest blow,
To think I'd never 'ave the chance to 'url them
    at the foe.
And there was all our boys in front, a-fightin'
    there like mad,
And me as could 'ave 'elped 'em wiv the lovely
    bombs I 'ad.
And so I cussed and cussed, and then I struggled
    back again,
Into that bit of battered trench, packed solid
    with its slain.

BILL THE BOMBER

Now as I lay a-lyin' there and blastin' of me lot,
And wishin' I could just dispose of all them
    bombs I'd got,
I sees within the doorway of a shy, retirin' dug-
    out
Six Boches all a-grinnin', and their Captain stuck
    'is mug out;
And they 'ad a nice machine gun, and I twigged
    what they was at,
And they fixed it on a tripod, and I watched 'em
    like a cat;
And they got it in position, and they seemed so
    werry glad,
Like they'd got us in a death-trap, which, con-
    demn their souls! they 'ad:
For there our boys was fightin' fifty yards in
    front, and 'ere
This lousy bunch of Boches they 'ad got us in the
    rear.

Oh! it set me blood a-boilin' and I quite forgot
    me pain;
So I started crawlin', crawlin' over all them
    mounds of slain;

BILL THE BOMBER

And them barstards was so busy like they 'ad no
    eyes for me,
And me bleedin' leg was draggin', but me right
    arm it was free . . .
And now they 'ave it all in shape, and swingin'
    sweet and clear,
And now they're all excited like, but—I am
    drawin' near;
And now they 'ave it loaded up, and now they're
    takin' aim . . .
Rat-tat-tat-tat! Oh here, says I, is where I join
    the game.
And my right arm it goes swingin', and a bomb
    it goes a-slingin',
And that "typewriter" goes wingin' in a thun-
    derbolt of flame.

Then those Boches, wot was left of them, they
    tumbled down their 'ole,
And up I climbed a mound of dead, and down on
    them I stole.
And oh! that blessèd moment when I heard their
    frightened yell,
And I laughed down in that dug-out, ere I bombed
    their souls to hell!

149

BILL THE BOMBER

And now I'm in the hospital, surprised that I'm
    alive.
We started out a thousand men, we came back
    thirty-five.
And I'm minus of a trotter, but I'm most amazin'
    gay,
For me bombs they wasn't wasted, though, you
    might say, "thrown away."

THE WHISTLE OF SANDY McGRAW

You may talk o' your lutes and your dulcimers
    fine,
  Your harps and your tabors and cymbals and a',
But here in the trenches jist gi'e me for mine,
  The wee penny whistle o' Sandy McGraw.
Oh! it's: "Sandy, ma lad, will you lilt us a tune?"
  And Sandy is willin' and trillin' like mad;
Sae silvery sweet that we a' throng aroun',
  And some o' it's gay, but the maist o' it's sad.
Jist the wee simple airs that sink intae your hert,
  And grup ye wi' love and wi' longin' for hame;
And ye glour like an owl till you're feelin' the
    stert
  O' a tear, and you blink wi' a feelin' o' shame.
For his song's o' the heather, and here in the dirt
  You listen and dream o' a land that's sae braw,
And he mak's you forget a' the harm and the hurt,
  For he pipes like a laverock, does Sandy
    McGraw.

*   *   *   *   *   *   *   *   *   *

THE WHISTLE OF SANDY McGRAW

At Eepers I mind me when rank upon rank
    We rose from the trenches and swept like the
        gale,
Till the rapid-fire guns got us fell on the flank
    And the murderin' bullets came swishin' like
        hail:
Till a' that were left o' us faltered and broke;
    Till it seemed for a moment a panicky rout,
When shrill through the fume and the flash and
        the smoke
    The wee valiant voice o' a whistle piped out
" *The Campbells are Comin'* ": Then into the fray
    We bounded wi' bayonets reekin' and raw,
And oh! we fair revelled in glory that day,
    Jist thanks to the whistle o' Sandy McGraw.

*   *   *   *   *   *   *   *   *

At Loose, it wis after a sconnersome fecht,
    On he field o' the slain I wis crawlin' aboot,
And the rockets were burnin' red holes in the
        nicht,
    And the guns they were veciously thunderin'
        oot.
When sudden I heard a bit sound like a sigh,
    And there in a crump-hole a kiltie I saw:
" Whit ails ye, ma lad? Are ye woundit?" says I.
    " I've lost ma wee whustle," says Sandy
        McGraw.

THE WHISTLE OF SANDY McGRAW

" 'Twas oot by yon bing where we pressed the
  attack,
  It drapped frae ma pooch, and between noo
  and dawn
There isna much time, so I'm jist crawlin' back."
  " Ye're daft, man!" I telt him, but Sandy wis
  gone.
Weel, I waited a wee, then I crawled oot masel',
  And the big stuff wis gorin' and roarin' around,
And I seemed tae be under the oxter o' hell,
  And creation wis crackin' tae bits by the sound,
And I says in ma mind: "Gang ye back, ye auld
  fule!"
  When I thrilled tae a note that wis saucy and
  sma';
And there in a crater, collected and cool,
  Wi' his wee penny whistle wis Sandy McGraw.
Ay, there he wis playin' as gleg as could be,
  And listenin' hard wis a spectacled Boche;
Then Sandy turned roon' and he noddit tae me,
  And he says: "Dinna blab on me, Sergeant
  McTosh.
The auld chap is deein'. He likes me tae play,
  It's makin' him happy. Jist see his een shine!"
And thrillin' and sweet in the hert o' the fray
  Wee Sandy wis playin' "*The Watch on the
  Rhine.*"

*   *   *   *   *   *   *   *   *

THE WHISTLE OF SANDY McGRAW

The last scene o' a',—'twas the day that we took
   That bit o' black ruin they ca' Labbiesell.
It seemed the hale hillside jist shivered and
   shook,
     And the red skies were roarin' and spewin' oot
     shell.
And the Sergeants were cursin' tae keep us in
   hand,
     And hard on the leash we were strainin' like
     dugs,
When upward we shot at the word o' command,
     And the bullets were dingin' their songs in oor
     lugs.
And onward we swept wi' a yell and a cheer,
     And a' wis destruction, confusion and din,
And we knew that the trench o' the Boches was
   near,
     And it seemed jist the safest bit hole tae be in.
So we a' tumbled doon, and the Boches were there,
     And they held up their hands, and they yelled:
     " Kamarad !"
And I marched aff wi' ten, wi' their palms in the
   air,
     And my, I was proodlike, and my! I was glad.
And I thocht: if ma lassie could see me jist
   then . . .
     When sudden I sobered at somethin' I saw,

THE WHISTLE OF SANDY McGRAW

And I stopped and I stared, and I halted ma men,
    For there on a stretcher wis Sandy McGraw.
Weel, he looks in ma face, jist as pert as ye please:
    "Ye ken hoo I hate tae be workin'," says he;
"But noo I can play in the street for bawbees,
    Wi' baith o' ma legs taken aff at the knee."
And though I could see he wis rackit wi' pain,
    He reached for his whistle and started tae play;
And quaverin' sweet wis the plaintive refrain:
    "The flo'ers o' the forest are a' wede away."
Then sudden he stoppit: "Man, wis it no' grand
    Hoo we took a' them trenches?" . . . He
      shakit his heid:
"I'll—no'—play—nae—mair—" feebly doon frae
    his hand
    Slipped the wee penny whistle and . . .
      Sandy wis deid.

  *   *   *   *   *   *   *   *   *

And so ye may talk o' your Steinways and Strads,
    Your wunnerfu' organs and brasses sae braw,
But oot in the trenches jist gi'e me, ma lads,
    Yon wee penny whistle o' Sandy McGraw.

THE STRETCHER-BEARER

My stretcher is one scarlet stain,
  And as I tries to scrape it clean,
I tell you wot,—I'm sick with pain
  For all I've 'eard, for all I've seen;
Around me is the 'ellish night,
  And as the war's red rim I trace,
I wonder if in 'Eaven's height,
  Our God don't turn away 'Is face.

I don't care 'ose the Crime may be;
  I holds no brief for kin or clan;
I 'ymns no 'ate; I only see
  As man destroys 'is brother man;
I waves no flag; I only know,
  As 'ere beside the dead I wait,
A million 'earts is weighed with woe,
  A million 'omes is desolate.

THE STRETCHER-BEARER

In dripping darkness, far and near,
　All night I've sought them woeful ones.
Dawn shudders up and still I 'ear
　The crimson chorus of the guns.
Look! like a ball of blood the sun
　'Angs o'er the scene of, wrath and wrong—
"Quick! Stretcher-bearers on the run!"
　O Prince of Peace! 'ow long, 'ow long?

WOUNDED

Is it not strange? A year ago to-day,
    With scarce a thought beyond the humdrum
        round,
I did my decent job and earned my pay;
    Was averagely happy, I'll be bound.
Ay, in my little groove I was content,
    Seeing my life run smoothly to the end,
With prosy days in stolid labour spent,
    And jolly nights, a pipe, a glass, a friend.
In God's good time a hearth-fire's cosy gleam,
    A wife and kids, and all a fellow needs;
When presto! like a bubble goes my dream:
    I leap upon the Stage of Splendid Deeds.
I yell with rage; I wallow deep in gore:
I, that was clerk in a drysalter's store.

Stranger than any book I've ever read:
    Here on the reeking battlefield I lie
Under the stars, propped up with smeary dead,
    Like, too, if no one takes me in, to die.

WOUNDED

Hit on the arms, legs, liver, lungs and gall;
  Damn glad there's nothing more of me to hit;
But calm, and feeling never pain at all,
  And full of wonder at the turn of it.
For of the dead around me three are mine,
  Three foemen vanquished in the whirl of fight;
So if I die I have no right to whine,
  I feel I've done my little bit all right;
I don't know how,—but there the beggars are,
As dead as herrings pickled in a jar.

And here am I, worse wounded than I thought;
  For in the fight a bullet bee-like stings;
You never heed; the air is metal-hot,
  And all alive with little flicking wings.
But on you charge. You see the fellows fall;
  Your pal was by your side, fair fighting-mad;
You turn to him, and lo! no pal at all;
  You wonder vaguely if he's copped it bad.
But on you charge. The heavens vomit death;
  And vicious death is besoming the ground.
You're blind with sweat; you're dazed, and out of
      breath,
  And though you yell, you cannot hear a sound.
But on you charge. Oh! War's a rousing game!
  Around you smoky clouds like ogres tower;
The earth is rowelled deep with spurs of flame,
  And on your helmet stones and ashes shower.

159

WOUNDED

But on you charge. It's odd! You have no fear.
  Machine-gun bullets whip and lash your path;
Red, yellow, black and smoky giants rear;
  The shrapnel rips, the heavens roar in wrath.
But on you charge. Barbed wire all trampled
    down,
  The ground all gored and rent as by a blast;
Grim heaps of grey where once were heaps of
    brown;
  A ragged ditch, the Hun first line at last.
All smashed to hell. Their second right ahead.
  So on you charge. There's nothing else to do.
More reeking holes, blood, barbed wire, gruesome
    dead;
  (Your puttee strap's undone,—that worries
    you.)
You glare around. You think you're all alone.
  But no; your chums come surging left and
    right.
The nearest chap flops down without a groan,
  His face still snarling with the rage of fight.
Ha! here's the second trench,—just like the first,
  Only a little more so, more "laid out";
More pounded, flame-corroded, death-accurst;
  A pretty piece of work, beyond a doubt.

WOUNDED

Now for the third, and there your job is done.
  So on you charge. You never stop to think.
Your cursèd puttee's trailing as you run;
  You feel you'd sell your soul to have a drink.
The acrid air is full of cracking whips.
  You wonder how it is you're going still.
You foam with rage. Oh God! to be at grips
  With someone you can rush and crush and kill.
Your sleeve is dripping blood; you're seeing red;
  You're battle-mad; your turn is coming now.
See! there's the jagged barbed wire straight ahead,
  And there's the trench,—you'll get there anyhow.
Your puttee catches on a strand of wire,
  And down you go; perhaps it saves your life,
For over sandbag rims you see 'em fire,
  Crop-headed chaps, their eyes ablaze with strife.
You crawl, you cower, then once again you plunge
  With all your comrades roaring at your heels.
Have at 'em, lads! You stab, you jab, you lunge;
  A blaze of glory, then the red world reels.
A crash of triumph, then . . . you're faint a bit . . .
  That cursèd puttee! Now to fasten it . . .

11   161

WOUNDED

Well, that's the charge, and now I'm here alone.
    I've built a little wall of Hun on Hun;
To shield me from the leaden bees that drone;
    (It saves me worry, and it hurts 'em none.)
The only thing I'm wondering is when
    Some stretcher-men will stroll along my way?
It isn't much that's left of me, but then
    Where life is, hope is, so at least they say.
Well, if I'm spared I'll be the happy lad,
    I tell you I won't envy any king.
I've stood the racket, and I'm proud and glad;
    I've had my crowning hour. Oh, War's the
        thing!
It gives us common, working chaps our chance,
    A taste of glory, chivalry, romance.

Ay, War, they say, is hell; it's heaven, too.
    It lets a man discover what he's worth.
It takes his measure, shows what he can do,
    Gives him a joy like nothing else on earth.
It fans in him a flame that otherwise
    Would flicker out, these drab and sordid
        days;
It teaches him in pain and sacrifice
    Faith, fortitude, grim courage past all praise.

WOUNDED

Yes, War is good. So here beside my slain,
  A happy wreck I wait amid the din,
For even if I perish mine's the gain . . .
  Hi there, you fellows! *Won't* you take me in?
Give me a fag to smoke upon the way . . .
  We've taken La Boiselle! The hell, you say!
Well, that would make a corpse sit up and
    grin . . .
  Lead on! I'll live to fight another day.

FAITH

Since all that is was ever bound to be;
    Since grim, eternal laws our Being bind;
    And both the riddle and the answer find,
And both the carnage and the calm decree;
Since plain within the Book of Destiny
    Is written all the journey of mankind
    Inexorably to the end; since blind
And mortal puppets playing parts are we:

Then let's have faith; good cometh out of ill;
    The power that shaped the strife shall end the
        strife;
Then let's bow down before the Unknown Will;
    Fight on, believing all is well with life;
Seeing within the worst of War's red rage,
The gleam, the glory of the Golden Age.

THE COWARD

'AVE you seen Bill's mug in the *Noos* to-day?
'E's gyned the Victoriar Cross, they say;
Little Bill wot would grizzle and run away,
    If you 'it 'im a swipe on the jawr.
'E's slaughtered the Kaiser's men in tons;
'E's captured one of their quick-fire guns,
And 'e 'adn't no practice in killin' 'Uns
    Afore 'e went off to the war.

Little Bill wot I nussed in 'is byby clothes;
Little Bill wot told me 'is childish woes;
'Ow often I've tidied 'is pore little nose
    Wiv the 'em of me pinnyfore.
And now all the papers 'is praises ring,
And 'e's been and 'e's shaken the 'and of the King,
And I sawr 'im to-day in the ward, pore thing,
    Where they're patching 'im up once more.

165

THE COWARD

And 'e says: " Wot d'ye think of it, Lizer Ann?"
And I says: " Well, I can't make it out, old man;
You'd 'ook it as soon as a scrap began,
    When you was a bit of a kid;"
And 'e whispers: " 'Ere, on the quiet, Liz,
They're makin' too much of the 'ole dam biz,
And the papers is printin' me ugly phiz,
    But . . . I'm 'anged if I know wot I did.

" Oh, the Captain comes and 'e says: ' Look 'ere!
They're far too quiet out there; it's queer.
They're up to somethin',—'oo'll volunteer
    To crawl in the dark and see?'
Then I felt me 'eart like a 'ammer go,
And up jumps a chap and 'e says: ' Right O !'
But I chips in straight, and I says, ' Oh, no !
    'E's a missis and kids,—take me!'

" And the next I knew I was sneakin' out,
And the oozy corpses was all about,
And I felt so scared I wanted to shout,
    And my skin fair prickled wiv fear;
And I sez: ' You coward! You 'ad no right
To take on the job of a man this night,'
Yet still I kept creepin' till ('orrid sight!)
    The trench of the 'Uns was near.

THE COWARD

" It was all so dark, it was all so still,
Yet somethin' pushed me against me will;
'Ow I wanted to turn! Yet I crawled until
    I was seein' a dim light shine.
Then thinks I: ' I'll just go a little bit,
And see wot the doose I can make of it,'
And it seemed to come from the mouth of a pit:
    ' Christmas!' sez I, ' a mine.'

" Then 'ere's the part wot I can't explain:
I wanted to make for 'ome again,
But somethin' was blazin' inside me brain,
    So I crawled to the trench instead;
Then I saw the bullet 'ead of a 'Un,
And 'e stood by a rapid-firer gun,
And I lifted a rock and I 'it 'im one,
    And 'e dropped like a chunk o' lead.

" Then all the 'Uns that was underground,
Comes up with a rush and on with a bound,
And I swings that giddy old Maxim round
    And belts 'em solid and square.
You see I was off me chump wiv fear,
' If I'm sellin' me life,' sez I, ' it's dear,'
And the trench was narrow and they was near,
    So I peppered the brutes for fair.

THE COWARD

" So I 'eld 'em back and I yelled with fright,
And the boys attacked and we 'ad a fight,
And we ' captured a section o' trench ' that night
    Which we didn't expect to get;
And they found me there with me Maxim gun,
And I'd laid out a score if I'd laid out one,
And I fainted away when the thing was done,
    And I 'aven't got over it yet."

So that's the 'istory Bill told me.
Of course it's all on the strict Q. T.;
It wouldn't do to get out, you see,
    As 'e hacted against 'is will.
But 'e's convalescin' wiv all 'is might,
And 'e 'opes to be fit for another fight;
Say! Ain't 'e a bit of the real, all right?
    Wot's the matter with Bill!

MISSIS MORIARTY'S BOY

Missis Moriarty called last week, and says she to
    me, says she:
"Sure the heart of me's broken entirely now;
    it's the fortunate woman you are;
You've still got your Dinnis to cheer up your
    home, but me Patsy boy, where is he?
Lyin' alone, cold as a stone, kilt in the weariful
    wahr.
Sure I'm seein' him now as I looked on him last,
    wid his hair all curly and bright,
And the wonderful, tenderful heart he had, and
    his eyes as he wint away,
Shinin' and lookin' down on me from the pride of
    his proper height:
Sure I'll remember me boy like that if I live till
    me dyin' day."

And just as she spoke them very same words me
    Dinnis came in at the door,
Come in from McGonigle's ould shebeen, came
    in from drinkin' his pay;
And Missis Moriarty looked at him, and she didn't
    say anny more,
And she wrapped her head in her ould black
    shawl, and she quietly wint away.

MISSIS MORIARTY'S BOY

And what was I thinkin', I ask ye now, as I put
    me Dinnis to bed?
  Wid him ravin' and cursin' one half of the
    night, as cold by his side I sat;
Was I thinkin' the poor ould woman she was wid
    her Patsy slaughtered and dead?
  Was I weepin' for Missis Moriarty? I'm not
    so sure about that.

Missis Moriarty goes about wid a shinin' look on
    her face,
  Wid her grey hair under her ould black shawl,
    and the eyes of her mother-mild;
Some say she's a little bit off her head, but anny-
    way it's the case,
  Her timper's so swate that you never would
    tell she'd be losin' her only child.
And I think, as I wait up every night for me
    Dinnis to come home blind,
  And I'm hearin' his stumblin' foot on the stair
    along about half-past three:
Sure there's many a way of breakin' a heart,—
    and I haven't made up me mind:
  Would I be Missis Moriarty, or Missis Moriarty
    me?

MY FOE

A Belgian priest-soldier speaks:

Gurr! You *cochon!* Stand and fight!
Show your mettle! Snarl and bite!
Spawn of an accursèd race,
Turn and meet me face to face!
Here amid the wreck and rout
Let us grip and have it out!
Here where ruins rock and reel
Let us settle steel to steel!
Look! Our houses, how they spit
Sparks from brands your friends have lit.
See! Our gutters running red,
Bright with blood your friends have shed.
Hark! Amid your drunken brawl
How our maidens shriek and call.
Why have *you* come here alone,
To this hearth's blood-spattered stone?
Come to ravish, come to loot,
Come to play the ghoulish brute.
Ah, indeed! We well are met,
Bayonet to bayonet.
God! I never killed a man:
Now I'll do the best I can.

MY FOE

Rip you to the evil heart,
Laugh to see the life-blood start.
Bah! You swine! I hate you so.
Show you mercy? No! . . . and no! . . .

There! I've done it. See! He lies
Death a-staring from his eyes;
Glazing eyeballs, panting breath,—
How it's horrible, is Death!
Plucking at his bloody lips
With his trembling finger-tips;
Choking in a dreadful way
As if he would something say
In that uncouth tongue of his . . .
Oh, how horrible Death is!

How I wish that he would die!
So unnerved, unmanned am I.
See! His twitching face is white!
See! His bubbling blood is bright.
Why do I not shout with glee?
What strange spell is over me?
There he lies; the fight was fair;
Let me toss my cap in air.
Why am I so silent? Why
Do I pray for him to die?
Where is all my vengeful joy?
Ugh! *My foe is but a boy.*

MY FOE

I'd a brother of his age
Perished in the war's red rage;
Perished in the Ypres hell:
Oh! I loved my brother well.
And though I be hard and grim,
How it makes me think of him!
He had just such flaxen hair
As the lad that's lying there.
Just such frank blue eyes were his   .   .   .
God! How horrible war is!

I have reason to be gay:
There is one less foe to slay.
I have reason to be glad:
Yet—my foe is such a lad.
So I watch in dull amaze,
See his dying eyes a-glaze,
See his face grow glorified,
See his hands outstretched and wide
To that bit of ruined wall
Where the flames have ceased to crawl,
Where amid the crumbling bricks
Hangs *a blackened crucifix.*

Now, oh! now I understand,
Quick I press it in his hand,
Close his feeble finger-tips,
Hold it to his faltering lips.

MY FOE

As I watch his welling blood
I would stem it if I could.
God of Pity, let him live!
God of Love, forgive, forgive!
 *   *   *   *   *   *   *   *

His face looked strangely, as he died,
Like that of One they crucified.
And in the pocket of his coat
I found a letter; thus he wrote:
The things I've seen! Oh mother, dear,
I'm wondering—can God be here?
To-night amid the drunken brawl
I saw a cross hung on a wall;
I'll seek it now, and there alone
Perhaps I may atone, atone.   .   .   .

Ah no! 'Tis I who must atone.
No other saw but God alone,
Yet how can I forget the sight
Of that face so woeful white?
Dead, I kissed him as he lay,
Knelt by him and tried to pray;
Left him lying there at rest,
Crucifix upon his breast.

Not for him the pity be:
Ye who pity, pity me,
Crawling now the ways I trod,
Blood-guilty in sight of God.

174

MY JOB

I'VE got a little job on 'and, the time is drawin'
   nigh,
   At seven by the Captain's watch I'm due to go
      and do it; .
I wants to 'ave it nice and neat, and pleasin' to
   the eye,
   And I 'opes the God of soldier men'll see me
      safely through it.
Because you see it's somethin' I 'ave never done
   before;
   And till you 'as experience noo stunts is always
      tryin';
The chances is I'll never 'ave to do it any more:
   At seven by the Captain's watch my little job
      is   .   .   .   *dyin'.*

I've got a little note to write, I'd best begin it
   now.
   I ain't much good at writin' notes, but here
      goes: "Dearest Mother,
I've been in many 'ot old 'does'; I've scraped
   through safe some'ow,
   But now I'm on the very point of tacklin' an-
      other.

MY JOB

A little job of hand-grenades; they called for vol-
    unteers.
  They picked me out: I'm proud of it; it seems
    a trifle dicky.
If anythin' should 'appen, well, there ain't no call
    for tears,
  And so . . .   I 'opes this finds you well.—
    Your werry lovin' Micky."

I've got a little score to settle wiv them swine out
    there.
  I've 'ad so many of me pals done in it's quite
    upset me.
I've seen so much of bloody death I don't seem for
    to care,
  If I can only even up, how soon the blighters
    get me.
I'm sorry for them perishers that corpses in a
    bed;
  I only 'opes mine's short and sweet, no linger-
    longer-lyin';
I made a mess of life, but now I'll try to make
    instead—
  It's seven sharp—good-bye, old pals! . . .
    a decent job in dyin',

THE SONG OF THE PACIFIST

WHAT do they matter, our headlong hates, when
    we take the toll of our Dead?
Think ye our glory and gain will pay for the tor-
    rent of blood we have shed?
By the cheers of our victory will the heart of the
    mother be comforted?

If by the victory all we mean is a broken and
    brooding foe;
Is the pomp and power of a glitt'ring hour, and
    a truce for an age or so:
By the clay-cold hand on the broken blade we
    have smitten a bootless blow!

If by the triumph we only prove that the sword
    we sheathe is bright;
That justice and truth and love endure; that
    Freedom's throned on the height;
That the feebler folks shall be unafraid; that
    Might shall never be Right;

THE SONG OF THE PACIFIST

If this be all: by the blood-drenched plains, by
the havoc of fire and fear,
By the rending roar of the War of Wars, by the
dead so doubly dear—
Then our victory is a vast defeat, and it mocks us
as we cheer.

Victory! there can be but one, hallowed in every
land:
When by the graves of our common dead we who
were foemen stand,
And in the hush of our common grief hand is ten-
dered to hand.

Triumph! Yes, when out of the dust in the splendour of their release
The spirits of those who fell go forth and they
hallow our hearts to peace,
And, brothers in pain, with world-wide voice, we
clamour that War shall cease.

Glory! Ay, when from blackest loss shall be born
most radiant gain;
When over the gory fields shall rise a star that
never shall wane:
Then and then only our dead shall know that they
have not fall'n in vain.

THE SONG OF THE PACIFIST

When our children's children shall talk of War
  as a madness that may not be;
When we thank our God for our grief to-day, and
  blazen from sea to sea
In the name of the dead the banner of Peace
  . . . *that will be Victory.*

THE TWINS

THERE were two brothers, John and James,
And when the town went up in flames,
To save the house of James dashed John,
Then turned, and lo! his own was gone.

And when the great World War began,
To volunteer John promptly ran;
And while he learned live bombs to lob,
James stayed at home and—sneaked his job.

John came home with a missing limb;
That didn't seem to worry him;
But oh! it set his brain awhirl
To find that James had—sneaked his girl!

Time passed.   John tried his grief to drown;
To-day James owns one half the town;
His Army Contracts riches yield;
And John?   Well, *search the Potter's Field.*

THE SONG OF THE SOLDIER-BORN

Give me the scorn of the stars and a peak defiant;
Wail of the pines and a wind with the shout of a
giant;
Night and a trail unknown, and a heart reliant.

Give me to live and love in the old, bold fashion,
A soldier's billet at night, and a soldier's ration,
A heart that leaps to the fight with a soldier's
passion.

For I hold as a simple faith, there's no denying,
The trade of a soldier's the only trade worth
plying;
The death of a soldier's the only death worth
dying.

So let me go, and leave your safety behind me;
Go the spaces of hazard, where nothing shall bind
me;
Go till the world is War, and then you will find
me.

THE SONG OF THE SOLDIER-BORN

Then you will call me and claim me, because you
    will need me;
Cheer me and gird me and into the battle-wrath
    speed me   .   .   .
And when it's over, spurn me, and no longer heed
    me.

For guile and a purse gold-greased are the arms
    you carry;
With deeds of paper you fight, and with pens you
    parry;
You call on the hounds of the law your foes to
    harry.

You with your: "Art for its own sake," posing
    and prinking;
You with your: "Live and be merry," eating and
    drinking;
You with your: "Peace at all hazard," from
    bright blood shrinking.

Fools! I will tell you now,—though the red rain
    patters,
And a million of men go down, it's little it mat-
    ters   .   .   .
There's the Flag up-flung to the stars, though it
    streams in tatters.

THE SONG OF THE SOLDIER-BORN

There's a glory gold never can buy to yearn and
    to cry for;
There's a hope that's as old as the sky to suffer
    and sigh for;
There's a faith that out-dazzles the sun to martyr
    and die for.

Ah, no! it's my dream that War will never be
    ended;
That men will perish like men, and valour be
    splendid;
That the Flag by the sword will be served, and
    honour defended.

That the tale of my fights will never be ancient
    story;
That though my eye may be dim and my beard be
    hoary,
I'll die as a soldier dies—on the Field of Glory.

So give me a strong right arm for a wrong's swift
    righting;
Stave of a song on my lips as my sword is smiting;
Death in my boots, maybe, but fighting, fighting.

AFTERNOON TEA

As I was saying . . . (No, thank you; I
    never take cream with my tea;
Cows weren't allowed in the trenches,—got out
    of the habit, y'see).
As I was saying, our Colonel leaped up like a
    youngster of ten:
"Come on, lads!" he shouts, "and we'll show
    'em," and he sprang to the head of the men.
Then some bally thing seemed to trip him, and he
    fell on his face with a slam . . .
Oh! he died like a true British soldier, and the
    last word he uttered was "Damn!"
And hang it! I loved the old fellow, and some-
    thing just burst in my brain,
And I cared no more for the bullets than I would
    for a shower of rain.
'Twas an awf'ly funny sensation (I say, this is
    jolly nice tea);
I felt as if something had broken; by gad! I was
    suddenly free.

AFTERNOON TEA

Free for a glorified moment, beyond regulations
    and laws,
Free just to wallow in slaughter, as the chap of
    the stone age was.

So on I went joyously nursing a Berserker rage
    of my own,
And though all my chaps were behind me, feeling
    most frightf'ly alone;
With the bullets and shells ding-donging, and the
    "krock" and the swish of the shrap;
And I found myself humming "Ben Bolt" . . .
    (Will you pass me the sugar, old chap?
Two lumps, please.) . . . What was I say-
    ing? Oh, yes, the jolly old dash;
We simply ripped through the barrage, and on
    with a roar and a crash.
My fellows, Old Nick couldn't stop 'em. On, on
    they went with a yell,
Till they tripped on the Boches' sand-bags—noth-
    ing much left to tell:
A trench so tattered and battered that even a rat
    couldn't live,
Some corpses tangled and mangled, wire you
    could pass through a sieve.

AFTERNOON TEA

The jolly old guns had bilked us, cheated us out
of our show,
And my fellows were simply yearning for a red
mix-up with the foe.
So I shouted to them to follow, and on we went,
roaring again,
Battle-tuned and exultant, on in the leaden rain.
Then all at once a machine gun barks from a bit
of a bank,
And our Major roars in a fury: "We've got to
take it on flank."
He was running like fire to lead us, when down
like a stone he comes,
As full of "type-writer" bullets as a pudding is
full of plums.
So I took his job and we got 'em . . . by
gad! we got 'em like rats;
Down in a deep shell-crater we fought like Kil-
kenny cats.
'Twas pleasant just for a moment to be sheltered
and out of range,
With someone you *saw* to go for,—it made an
agreeable change.

And the Boches that missed my bullets, my chaps
    gave a bayonet jolt,
And all the time, I remember, I whistled and
    hummed " Ben Bolt."
Well, that little job was over, so hell-for-leather
    we ran,
On to the second line trenches—that's where the
    fun began.
For though we had strafed 'em like fury, there
    still were some Boches about,
And my fellows, teeth set and eyes glaring, like
    terriers routed 'em out.
Then I stumbled on one of their dug-outs, and I
    shouted : " Is anyone there?"
And a voice, " Yes, one; but I'm wounded," came
    faint up the narrow stair;
And my man was descending before me, when
    sudden a cry ! a shot !
(I say, this cake is delicious.   You make it your-
    self, do you not?)
My man?   Oh! they killed the poor devil; for if
    there was one there was ten;
So after I'd bombed 'em sufficient I went down at
    the head of my men,
And four tried to sneak from a bunk-hole, but we
    cornered the rotters all right;
I'd rather not go into details, 'twas messy that bit
    of the fight.

But all of it's beastly messy; let's talk of pleas-
    anter things,
The skirts that the girls are wearing, ridiculous
    fluffy things,
So short that they show . . . Oh. hang it!
    Well, if I must, I must:
We cleaned out the second trench line, bomb and
    bayonet thrust,
And on we went to the third one, quite calloused
    to crumping by now;
And some of our fellows who'd passed us were
    making a deuce of a row;
And my chaps, well, I just couldn't hold 'em;
    (it's strange how it is with gore;
In some ways it's just like whiskey: if you taste
    it you must have more.)
Their eyes were like beacons of battle; by gad,
    sir! they couldn't be calmed,
So I headed 'em bang for the bomb-belt, racing
    like billy-be-damned.
Oh! it didn't take long to arrive there, those who
    arrived at all;
The machine-guns were certainly chronic, the
    shindy enough to appal.
Oh, yes, I omitted to tell you, I'd wounds on the
    chest and the head,
And my shirt was torn to a gun-rag, and my face
    blood-gummy and red.

AFTERNOON TEA

I'm thinking I looked like a madman; I fancy I
felt one, too,
Half naked and swinging a rifle . . . God!
what a glorious "do."
As I sit here in old Piccadilly, sipping my after-
noon tea,
I see a blind, bullet-chipped devil, and it's hard to
believe that it's me:
I see a wild, war-damaged demon, smashing out
left and right,
And humming "Ben Bolt" rather loudly, and
hugely enjoying the fight.
And as for my men, may God bless 'em! I've
loved 'em ever since then:
They fought like the shining angels; they're the
pick o' the land, my men.
And the trench was a reeking shambles, not a
Boche to be seen alive—
So I thought—but on rounding a traverse I came
on a covey of five;
And four of 'em threw up their flippers, but the
fifth chap, a sergeant, was game,
And though I'd a bomb and revolver he came at
me just the same.
A sporty thing that, I tell you; I just couldn't
blow him to hell,
So I swung to the point of his jaw-bone, and
down like a nine-pin he fell.

AFTERNOON TEA

And then when I'd brought him to reason, he
    wasn't half bad, that Hun;
He bandaged my head and my short-rib as well
    as the Doc. could have done.
So back I went with my Boches, as gay as a two-
    year-old colt,
And it suddenly struck me as rummy—I still was
    a-humming " Ben Bolt."
And now, by Jove! how I've bored you. You've
    just let me babble away:
Let's talk of the things that *matter*—your car or
    the newest play.

THE MOURNERS

I LOOK into the aching womb of night;
  I look across the mist that masks the dead;
The moon is tired and gives but little light,
    The stars have gone to bed.

The earth is sick and seems to breathe with pain;
  A lost wind whimpers in a mangled tree;
I do not see the foul, corpse-cluttered plain,
    The dead I do not see.

The slain I *would* not see . . . and so I lift
  My eyes from out the shambles where they lie;
When lo! a million woman-faces drift
    Like pale leaves through the sky.

The cheeks of some are channelled deep with tears;
  But some are tearless, with wild eyes that stare
Into the shadow of the coming years
    Of fathomless despair.

THE MOURNERS

And some are young, and some are very old;
 And some are rich, some poor beyond belief;
Yet all are strangely like, set in the mould
  Of everlasting grief.

They fill the vast of Heaven, face on face;
 And then I see one weeping with the rest,
Whose eyes beseech me for a moment's space . . .
  Oh! eyes I love the best!

Nay, I but dream. The sky is all forlorn,
 And there's the plain of battle writhing red:
God pity them, the women-folk who mourn!
  How happy are the dead.

L'ENVOI

My job is done: my rhymes are ranked and ready,
  My word-battalions marching verse by verse;
Here stanza-companies are none too steady,
  There print-platoons are weak, but might be
    worse:
And as in marshalled order I review them,
  My type-brigades, unfearful of the fray,
My eyes that seek their faults are seeing through
    them
  Immortal visions of an epic day.

It seems I'm in a giant bowling-alley:
  The hidden heavies round me crash and thud;
A spire snaps like a pipe-stem in the valley,
  The rising sun is like a ball of blood.
Along the road the fantassins are pouring,
  And some are gay as fire, and some steel-
    stern . . .
Then back again I see the red tide pouring
  Along the reeking road from Hebuterne.

L'ENVOI

And once again I seek Hill Sixty-seven,
  The Hun lines grey and peaceful in my sight;
When suddenly the rosy air is riven—
  A " coal-box " blots the boyou on my right.
Or else to evil Carnoy I am stealing,
  Past sentinels who hail with bated breath;
Where not a cigarette spark's dim revealing
  May hint our mission in that zone of death.

I see across the shrapnel-seeded meadows
  The jaggèd rubble-heap of La Boiselle;
Blood-guilty Fricourt brooding in the shadows,
  And Thiepval's château empty as a shell.
Down Albert's riven streets the moon is leering;
  The hanging Virgin takes its bitter ray;
And all the road from Hamel I am hearing
  The silver rage of bugles over Bray.

Once more within the sky's deep sapphire hollow
  I see a swimming Taube, a fairy thing;
I watch the angry shell flame flash and follow
  In feather puffs that flick a tilted wing;
And then it fades, with shrapnel mirror's flash-
      ing;
  The flashes bloom to blossoms lily gold;
The batteries are rancorously crashing,
  And life is just as full as it can hold.

194

L'ENVOI

Oh! spacious days of glory and of grieving!
  Oh! sounding hours of lustre and of loss;
Let us be glad we lived you, still believing
  The God who gave the cannon gave the Cross.
Let us not doubt amid these seething passions,
  The lusts of blood and hate our souls abhor:
The Power that Order out of Chaos fashions
  Smites fiercest in the wrath-red forge of
    War . . .
Have faith! Fight on! Amid the battle hell
Love triumphs, Freedom beacons, all is well.